DONATION

CONDUCTING FUNDAMENTALS

CONDUCTING FUNDAMENTALS

STANLEY LINTON
University of Wisconsin, Oshkosh

Prentice-Hall, Inc., Englewood Cliffs, N.J. 07632

Library of Congress Cataloging in Publication Data

Linton, Stanley.
  Conducting fundamentals.

  Includes indexes.
  1. Conducting. I. Title.
MT85.L615   781.6'35   81-13900
ISBN 0-13-167320-3   AACR2

Editorial/production supervision
  and interior design by Joyce Turner
Cover design by Wanda Lubelska
Manufacturing buyer: Harry P. Baisley
Page makeup by Diane Heckler Koromhas
  and Debra Watson

I wish to express my appreciation to Thomas W. Herzing
who edited the original manuscript.

Printed in the United States of America
10 9 8 7 6 5 4 3 2 1

ISBN 0-13-167320-3

Prentice-Hall International, Inc., *London*
Prentice-Hall of Australia Pty. Limited, *Sydney*
Prentice-Hall of Canada, Ltd., *Toronto*
Prentice-Hall of India Private Limited, *New Delhi*
Prentice-Hall of Japan, Inc., *Tokyo*
Prentice-Hall of Southeast Asia Pte. Ltd., *Singapore*
Whitehall Books Limited, *Wellington, New Zealand*

Contents

Hemiola, 166

Preface

This book has been written to, and for, those who seek to gain the fundamental specialized knowledge and skills necessary to conduct music in rehearsal and performance. It can serve as a primary instructional resource for students in conducting classes, for relatively inexperienced practicing conductors, and for individuals who want to learn about conducting techniques through independent study.

A basic assumption underlying this book is that foundations for effective conducting are built on competent musicianship, disciplined technique, and applications of musicianship and technique within the expressive contexts of a variety of music. No distinction in kinds of basic needs is made by idiom (choral or instrumental), so this book can be used by anyone preparing to function as conductor of a band, a choir, an orchestra, or any other type of musical ensemble.

The book's scope, sequential organization, and use of various print media are inseparably interrelated. It starts with the premise that the user has a functional ability to read and perform music but has little or no formal knowledge or experience in conducting. Instructional chapters one and two provide an orientation to the role of the conductor and to the physical elements of conducting movement. Chapters three, four, and five provide a foundation in conducting technique, which is critical to each individual's continued progress. These three chapters focus on conducting in a three-beat pattern in ways that will lead to employing well-formed patterns of movement and applying techniques and gestures (including independent uses of the left hand) that will communicate dynamics, styles of articulation, on-beat attacks, entrance cues, points of stress or relaxation, releases, fermatas, and phrase shapes. Years of teaching beginners have led me to a conviction that a three-beat pattern is excellent for early conducting experiences, first, because its correct and expressive forms can be achieved with relative ease, and second, because it includes both the vertical and lateral directions, which provide a sound base for development of all fundamental movements and gestures.

Chapters six to twelve build upon the knowledge and skills established in chapters three to five. They extend the learner's experiences through all beat patterns in simple meters, compound meters, irregular meters, and changing meters with either constant or variable beat units; through after-beat attacks and divided-beat patterns; and through conducting special musical events such as accents, syncopation, cross rhythms, and hemiola patterns. All twelve instructional chapters are sequenced in such a way as to introduce new material as the learner is able to handle it and to allow the student to continue applying what has been learned as new knowledge and technique are being presented. In total, the material covered includes all of the basic techniques needed to conduct almost any kind of event found in a music score in traditional notation.

One of the main themes of this book is the conductor's responsibility to apply disciplined, well-formed conducting movements both to control ensemble precision and to communicate aesthetic values in the music. The means of shaping phrases, for instance, are given attention from almost the beginning of the study of technique. Both verbal and nonverbal materials are employed in presenting the concepts and skills that lead to the goal of disciplined and expressive conducting. The written presentations of rationales, definitions, descriptions, and analyses are supported and illustrated by photographs that picture physical factors, numerous drawings that show the forms of all basic conducting movements, nonpitch (notated) exercises that supply resources for practicing specific skills, and excerpts from music that provide opportunities to analyze, understand, and apply what is being learned about conducting.

Special reference should be made to the 125 musical examples. Each excerpt serves a dual purpose: It illustrates a concept or technique and provides a musical context for application of ideas and skills. Failure to actually practice conducting these examples is an underutilization of the book's resources. The musical examples represent orchestral, band, and choral literature; many are from familiar music. Their forms range from a single voice line to all parts condensed on two or more staves. But in all cases the excerpt contains the elements necessary for meaningful study and practice. Each is accompanied by a brief conducting analysis, which includes references to specific points in the score that may need a conductor's attention and identifies techniques to apply in doing so. If the suggestions sometimes seem too detailed, we prefer in those cases to err on the side of overspecificity, since most beginners need a fairly high level of prescribed activities to try and do in order to develop a pool of functional technique from which to make choices and decisions about conducting. Most of the examples are relatively easy to perform by singing or playing them; they offer opportunities for conducting short, live performances.

This book, then, is more than a treatise on "baton technique" or "time beating." It is intended especially to help the beginner, from his earliest experiences, establish attitudes, insights, and skills for becoming (through continued study and experience) a truly competent musical performer as a conductor.

Acknowledgment and appreciation are given to the following: To the publishers whose credit lines appear with the musical examples quoted, to Claude N. Pensis for photography, to Henri B. Pensis for photographic poses, to Bruce Wise for his assistance in editing and proofreading musical examples, and to my wife, Hope, for her help in proofreading the final manuscript and for her toleration of a preoccupied husband.

Stanley Linton

CONDUCTING FUNDAMENTALS

Model for Score Preparation

INTRODUCTION

You are beginning to study conducting, and a good starting point is to consider some basic assumptions that provide us with a common frame of reference and a similar point of view. The first assumption is that conducting is an applied musical medium; it is a kind of musical performance. You are the primary performer, and the orchestra, choir, or band is your instrument. Performing as a conductor is both different from and similar to other mediums of musical performance. The main difference is that the conductor is removed from direct contact with the source of sound and, instead, depends on the responses of other performers to recreate a piece of music. For this reason a conductor must communicate effectively with the players or singers. Verbal communication is needed at various times during rehearsal, and nonverbal communication is always used in rehearsal and public performance. Motions and gestures of the arms, hands, and baton, along with body stance and facial expression, are the vehicles for nonverbal communication and are the primary skills you must learn in order to conduct.

There are also similarities between conducting and other kinds of musical performance. Competent conducting is based, first of all, on fundamental musicianship—knowledge, skill, and feeling. We must assume that you have some degree of skill in reading music, that you have had experience in listening to music and performing music with your voice or an instrument, that you have had or are in the process of acquiring a background in music theory and history, and that you are growing in your musical understanding and sensitivity through all of your musical activities. Conducting, like other areas of performance, has its own body of specialized knowledge and techniques, which can be learned best when there is a musical foundation upon which to build. All conductors should be solid musicians, but being a good musician will not of itself make you a good conductor. Satisfactory progress toward competency in conducting requires meaningful practice of the techniques and their continued application to music and with musical ensembles.

A second assumption is that fundamental concepts and techniques of conducting are the same, regardless of whether the musical idiom is instrumental or vocal: whether the ensemble is a choir, an orchestra, or a band. Sometimes people have assumed—invalidly—that the style varies with the idiom, usually as a result of observing certain choral conductors who demonstrate an extremely free, loose, undisciplined style and certain instrumental conductors who exhibit the opposite extreme in a style that is precise, metronomic, unyielding, and stiff. Conducting should be both disciplined and expressive. When you apply primary techniques to different idioms, therefore, you merely adapt to the musical score and the ensemble you conduct.

The final assumption is that the best model of conducting technique for you as a beginning student is one that is physically well-coordinated, clear in its communication of important musical events, responsive to expressive values in the music, and visually acceptable to observers. You should learn from your observations of other conductors without attempting to copy all you see. Some experienced conductors have developed bad habits that result in sloppy, vague, or superfluous motion. Many professional conductors, on the other hand, have developed highly personalized styles that would not function for you as well as for them. Your own individual style will develop over time and with increasing experience, but in the beginning most techniques and their applications should be approached and practiced in specified ways. Furthermore, a review of the fundamentals from time to time is just as important for the conductor as it is for any skilled performer.

This textbook will introduce you to fundamental concepts and skills that can serve as the basis for effective conducting with any kind of ensemble and with most music of the Western world of any historical period from Renaissance to contemporary. Various beat patterns and conducting motions used to control important musical events are given verbal descriptions and rationales; they also are represented in photographs and drawings and illustrated with musical examples and practice exercises. Your developing technique (under the supervision of your instructor) will follow a growth pattern intrinsic to the sequence and content of the instructional units. To gain a sense of what it is like to function as a conductor, you must go beyond what is presented in the text and take opportunities, in class and out of class, to conduct live sound and complete pieces of music.

MUSICAL ANALYSIS

The ultimate goal in studying conducting is to acquire an ability to apply basic musicianship and conducting skills while conducting a live rehearsal or public performance of a piece of music. An essential part of the entire process that leads toward this goal can be called "score preparation," a broad term that means thoroughly learning the music from the standpoint of a conductor. A general model for score preparation might include the components of score reading, musical analysis, conducting analysis, and conducting practice. These elements are considered in this first chapter, but the ideas presented are ones that you should review throughout your study and ones that will take on increased meaning with each new application.

Competent conducting requires comprehensive musicianship on the part of the conductor. Interpretation of the musical score is an act of integrated musicianship and the governor of conducting technique. Perception and conceptualization of the composite score comes from applying one's combined knowledge and experience in music theory, history, literature, and performance. Bad conducting can result from either weak musicianship or inadequate technique.

You should make a broad musical analysis (and sometimes a detailed one) of the score you are preparing to conduct, either after or while gaining an acquaintance with its sound. During your analysis you might consider the answers to the following questions about how sound is organized in the piece.

Rhythmic Organization

What is the beat unit, the meter, and the tempo? Are there changes in tempo or meter?

Are there rhythmic motives that characterize the piece, or a major section of it?

Are there places where the composite rhythm requires particularly clear movement in the individual voice lines?

Where, and in what voice lines, are the points of greatest rhythmic activity or complexity?

Where do the voice lines move in synchronous (same in all parts) patterns, and where is there greater independence between the patterns?

At what points might the entrance of a voice line require the attention of the conductor (for example, initial entrance, following a long silence)?

Pitch Organization and Texture

What are the important features of the tonality—key, mode, clear or ambiguous tonal centers, important modulations?

What kinds of phrase contours are involved, and where are these of particular importance in shaping the phrases?

Is the pitch movement in the various voice lines characterized by conjunct (steps) or disjunct (skips) motion?

Are there certain chords or chord progressions that need further analysis?

In what voice part or parts do you find the melodic-thematic material?

Is the texture primarily homophonic, polyphonic, or some combination of the two?

Is the harmonic content relatively consonant or dissonant? Are there places where dissonance, such as a suspension, might need special attention from the conductor?

If the music is polyphonic, is the contrapuntal treatment of voice lines imitative or nonimitative? If homophonic, are there important melodic patterns in the voice lines supporting the primary melody?

Form

What is the outer (overall) form (for example, binary, ternary, through-composed, motet, fugue, theme and variations, sonata-allegro)?

Where does each phrase cadence? Is the cadence synchronous (same point in all parts) or overlapping (different points)? Which cadences need harmonic analysis and identification (half, authentic, plagal, deceptive)?

Do the phrases relate or unite into larger identifiable units of design such as sentences, phrase groups, or major parts or sections?

Are the smaller units of design more in the form of motives, or melodic-rhythmic fragments, instead of normal phrases? If so, where are they found in the score at any given time, and how does this structure affect the music's aesthetic qualities?

What features provide unity and variety in the form?

Where are the compositional procedures of repetition, contrast, imitation, or variation significant to the technical-aesthetic-dramatic content of the piece?

Style

In what historical period was the piece composed?

In what ways (if any) does the style of that period affect such things as tempo, dynamics, and articulation in performing the piece?

How is the individual style of the composer reflected in the piece?

Dynamic Scheme

What stable levels of loudness (for example, *forte, piano*) are marked throughout the piece?

Where are variable dynamics (for example, *crescendo, diminuendo)* marked?

Where does the primary climax occur? Where are the secondary climaxes?

Text in Choral Music

What is the essence of the meaning and feeling of the entire text when read apart from the music?

What are the important words in each phrase?

Has the connotation, or the sense of stress-relaxation, of certain words been reinforced in their musical treatment (e.g., word painting, relative duration, melisma, type of chord)?

CONDUCTING ANALYSIS

After acquiring an aural-visual familiarity with the score and making an initial musical analysis of the piece, you should study the score from the standpoint of conducting requirements. Below are some types of decisions that should be made regarding how to conduct various passages and what techniques to apply.

Decisions about Beat Unit and Tempo

The basis for determining what kind of note should function as the beat unit (one beat's duration) and what conducting pattern should be used is introduced in Chapter Three and continued in applications to various meters and musical examples through subsequent chapters. Setting the correct tempo at the beginning of a piece is the sole responsibility of the conductor. Four primary criteria can be used in arriving at the "right" speed:

Metronome marking. A metronome marking is a concrete and exact reference to the number of a certain kind of note that should occur per minute. A marking of $\downarrow$ = 120 means 120 quarter notes, or quarter-note beats, per minute, which is at a rate of two per second. Another interpretation could be that half-note beats would be at the rate of 60 per minute or one per second. Such an indication included in the written score provides an excellent guide to the proper tempo, assuming it was carefully determined by the composer or editor in the first place. However, in certain known instances even the composer does not perform the passage according to the exact metronome marking he or she supplied in the printed score.

Tempo terms. Words that suggest an intended fixed tempo are found at the beginning of most scores, and these terms are frequently the traditional Italian words listed at the end of this chapter. A tempo term alone provides a valuable, but only general, clue to the exact speed for the music. An *Allegro* in one piece may be considerably faster than in another (*Allegro* in a twentieth-century style, for example, is probably more lively than a Baroque *Allegro*).

Tradition. If a piece has a history and tradition of performance by reputable conductors, knowledge of this tradition contributes to setting a good tempo. Listening to live or recorded performances of a work will help you make your own decision, but you should be aware that variances in the exact speed do occur among different conductors performing the same work and among different performances of a work by the same conductor.

Feel of the tempo. Markings, terms, and tradition can provide a close approximation of the right tempo for a given piece. But in making a final judgment, the conductor must also determine an exact tempo that feels best for that piece, and this can be accomplished by answering such questions as these: At what tempo does the spirit of the music (and the text in choral music) achieve its maximum aesthetic potential? What tempo maintains the best feeling of forward movement of the sounds—the point where quicker movement would feel unpoised and slower movement would cause a sense of gradual loss of momentum and intensity? At what tempo can the quickest patterns in the piece be articulated adequately? At what tempo can the clarity of all parts be maintained at all times?

Other Decisions

Dynamics. The opening level of loudness and all subsequent points at which significant changes occur should be clearly identified in the score and kept in mind so that the necessary changes in length and weight of the beat pattern can be anticipated and timed properly.

Articulation. Make a somewhat detailed analysis of the types of articulation (legato, staccato, marcato) required for the best performance of various passages in the piece so that the most appropriate style of beat will be deliberately employed at those places in the score.

Durations. Find the places in the score where the composite rhythm is of most importance and other places where particular patterns in single voice lines are more significant. The conductor must sometimes give primary attention to rhythmic events.

Attacks and releases. Locate points in the score where clear preparation for and timing of precise attacks and releases will become of primary concern in order for the conductor to control them during rehearsal and performance. Determine the kind of conducting motion that will function best for each.

Cues. Identify places in the score where the conductor will need to give a cue for the entrance of a voice part. Such cues are customarily given at the first entrance of a part, after a long rest, when a voice line starts important melodic or rhythmic material, or when the attack is tricky or difficult.

Special effects and problems. Study the score to determine where special circumstances interrupt or alter the ongoing events in such a way as to require special gestures by the conductor. Such situations include accents, breaks, fermatas, and cross rhythms. Conducting techniques to handle these circumstances will be introduced in subsequent chapters.

SCORE READING

Score reading for the conductor, as for any performer, involves the combined aural-visual skills required to relate the written score and the sounds it represents. Notes are merely a visual stimulus and their sound an auditory stimulus, both of which must be processed through the brain into the neuromuscular responses that make up the conducting motions. In one way or another, the written score must be seen with perceptions that will enable the conductor to anticipate and expect the composite sound and its more important components in advance of the actual occurrence. Many performers have developed the habit of concentrating on only one linear voice line. As conductors, however, they must quickly break this habit and replace it with one of seeing vertical-horizontal blocks of the entire score. The vertical dimension includes all voice lines and all staves on which they are notated. Horizontal (linear) aspects could be of any scope from one chord to one measure to one complete phrase or more.

The conductor's view of blocks of the written score might not include all specific details, and especially not every single pitch or rhythmic duration, for a conductor never communicates specific pitch and only infrequently communicates single time values. Most beginning conductors will acquire a sense of the aggregate sound of a music score in preparation for conducting by playing it at a keyboard instrument or listening to a recording of the piece. Beginners should also attempt to hear silently (mentally) as much of the combined sound as possible. Thorough familiarity with the sound and sight of individual voice lines is also important and contributes to a perception of the composite score. Try singing and/or playing voice lines separately and playing various combinations of two or three parts.

Reference to the Score

Whether a conductor ultimately conducts with a score or without one (from memory) is an individual decision. Use of a score is always acceptable; it is a necessity for the beginner. You should become so familiar with the aural-visual components of the score that the page of notation serves only as a reminder of the expected sounds when you give brief glances, as needed, at blocks of the page of notation. The following points are useful guidelines for referring to the score while conducting it:

1. Look at the score only when necessary to remind yourself of what musical events are to be anticipated over the next several beats or measures. Each glance should take no more than one to three seconds.
2. See a vertical-horizontal block of the total score along with the important details that need communication through conducting motions.
3. Shift eye contact (the field of vision) back and forth from the ensemble to the score. Eye contact with the performers should occupy more of your time than looking at the written page.
4. Maintain eye contact with the performers, instead of the score, in important situations such as:
   a. during the preparatory stance and initial attack, and at the final release ending the piece or a major section
   b. at cadences: the ending of one phrase and beginning of the next
   c. at points where important cues are to be given (for example, entrance of a voice, passing of the melody to another voice, a break or fermata, an important rhythmic or melodic pattern)
   d. at changes in the ongoing tempo or dynamic level.

5. Turn the page, with the left hand, several beats before or after the sound arrives at that point. Choose an exact moment when cues or other special gestures are not involved.

Musical Examples

The following three excerpts from musical scores illustrate some important items for a conductor to see while conducting the passages. Composite blocks are enclosed with horizontal and vertical broken lines delineating a field to be viewed as quickly as possible and ahead of its production by the players or singers.

Scores for four-part mixed chorus with piano, or without instrumental accompaniment, are among the easiest to read. The normal present-day form for printing choral music employs a separate staff for each voice part and the great staff for the piano part. All staves are connected ahead of the clef signs by a vertical line, and the voice parts are further grouped by a heavy line called a brace; the piano music is separated by a brace of another style (see Musical Example 1–1). Soprano, alto, and tenor parts are usually written in G clef (treble clef) and the bass voice part in F clef (bass clef), although in some scores C clefs are used for all but the bass line. You should realize at all times that a male voice reading from G clef is a transposing instrument sounding an octave lower than written; therefore, play the tenor part an octave lower when reproducing it on a keyboard instrument.

So-called *A Cappela* music for unaccompanied voices usually has a piano part (for rehearsal only) that is a duplication of the voice parts. This kind of score should be studied by playing the piano part as well as various voice combinations from the "open" score comprising the separate vocal staves. If the piano part is an independent accompaniment, study the chorus parts and piano part both separately and together.

Musical Example 1–1 is for mixed chorus, with orchestra parts reduced and condensed for piano. The collective sound is relatively easy to learn by playing the piano score because it doubles the vocal parts. For this same reason, the conductor would probably give primary attention to the chorus. If you have learned the music well, reference to the written score during performance could be based on these suggestions:

1. Have at least the first three measures well in mind before making the initial attack, including the opening tempo, legato style, dynamic level, and the *crescendo-diminuendo* that shapes the phrase.
2. Keep eye contact with the ensemble until after cuing the bass attack on count 3 in measure 3; then glance back at the score to remind yourself that in measures 4–6 there is a phrasing in all parts with count 4, measure 4, and a gradual *crescendo* through the next phrase (measures 5 and 6) to a *forte* on the word *end* where a release of the phrase occurs in count 4.
3. Look ahead, during the *crescendo*, into the next system of staves to remind yourself of the *piano* imitative entrances at two-count intervals in the sequence of tenor, alto, soprano, and bass. Eye contact should remain with

the ensemble during the *forte* release of "end" and the following entrances of voice lines.

4. A quick glance back at the score following the bass entrance (measure 8) will help you recall that the tenor and soprano lines restate the "shall be saved" motive (partially augmented in duration), and that following a *crescendo* the alto section restates the opening phrase "He that shall endure to the end" at a *forte* level beginning on count 1, measure 11.

5. Finally, look again as soon as the altos have been cued to attack in measure 11 and see that the soprano and alto parts cadence at the end of measure 12 while the tenor part is overlapping into measure 13.

MUSICAL EXAMPLE 1–1. **Mendelssohn, Eiljah, No. 32, He That Shall Endure, beginning measures.**

Staves carrying the various lines in a conductor's score for orchestra are arranged vertically from top to bottom according to families of instruments, with woodwinds at the top followed down the page by brass, percussion, and strings (Musical Example 1–2). Arrangement within each family is from highest to lowest (except in the brass family, where horn parts appear above trumpets). Thus, flutes have the top staff and bassoons the bottom staff in the woodwind group. Each family also is set apart visually by a heavy brace, and when more than one staff is needed to write parts for the same instrument (Violin 1 and 2), a second brace is added. Bar lines between measures are solid through all staves in a family and break between families. Information of the kind necessary to deal with clefs, transpositions, and instrumentation in orchestra and band scores is included in Appendixes A, B, and C. However, skill in applying this knowledge can best be gained by practicing with actual scores selected by your teacher and under his or her direction.

Your study of Musical Example 1–2 might include, from your previous analysis of the complete work, knowledge that: 1) the score is for a typical instrumentation of the orchestra of Haydn and Mozart (plus clarinets); 2) the third movement is in minuet form; 3) minuet form comprises two three-part (A-B-A) song forms with the second labeled *Trio*; and 4) the page quoted contains the end of Part A and the beginning of Part B of the first song form. Familiarity with the sound of the music could be gained by listening to a recorded or live performance of the work while following the written score, and by silently studying (and later playing on a piano) parts singly and in various combinations.

Details within blocks of the score in Musical Example 1–2 that you should note and attend to as a conductor include the following:

1. During the repetition of Part A, you should be anticipating its ending at a *forte* level with a final cadence in all parts on count 1 preceding the double bar. Release of this chord should be directed to the entire ensemble.

2. A glance at the score during the first measure of the page would remind you of the sequence of events that begin Part B at the double bar: a *piano* attack of a two-measure motive on count 3 in the violins, a two-measure answer in the oboes and horns, a two-measure restatement (a fourth higher) in the violins, and a *forte* answer in the high woodwinds and violins with the cellos, basses, and bassoons making their first entrance one measure later on count 3. You can train yourself to retain all of this without looking back at the score or, if necessary, take a quick look at about the third measure from the end of the page. You should be aware of the timpani and clarinet lines, but your primary attention should be given to cuing parts with the melodic material.

Concert band scores are a product of the twentieth century. Most that have been published within recent years include both a full and condensed conductor's score. Full scores are frequently larger than orchestra scores and might include as

MUSICAL EXAMPLE 1–2. Haydn, Symphony No. 101 in D Major (Clock), Movement III, measures 26–35.

many as twenty-four separate staffs, because of the addition of various sizes of clarinets and saxophones, inclusion of both cornets and trumpets, and the multiplicity of percussion instruments.

A condensed score usually consists of three or four staves, with each staff carrying one to three or four instrumental parts. A further characteristic is that all parts are written in C so that the actual sounds of both transposing and nontransposing instruments are as written. Indication of which instruments are on each staff is given as clearly as possible. Condensed scores make the preparatory study of composite sound easier, because the main framework can be played on a piano. Experienced conductors, of course, prefer the full score, but the condensed form will serve our present purpose adequately.

Analysis of the opening measures in Musical Example 1–3 reveals a four-note harmonic motive (staves two and three) that is repeated in ostinato fashion throughout the excerpt. Variations in the repetitions are interesting. Instruments starting on the second from top staff move in parallel inverted triads with marcato (accented) articulation at a *forte* level. Dissonance and greater intensity are created through addition of the baritone (third staff), which moves in parallel ninths with the top voice. Each repetition of the motive changes in articulation from marcato to tenuto to staccato to legato, and by the fourth measure the dissonant interval has been omitted and the level of loudness has dropped to *mezzo forte*.

You should refer to the score (Musical Example 1–3) before giving the opening attack. Retention of the entire passage, without further reference until the fourth or fifth measure, can be accomplished by remembering the following sequence of events:

1. *Forte* opening attack on the downbeat in the bass instruments
2. Attack of the four-note motive in other instruments on beat 2 and continuation in marcato style
3. Change to tenuto style on beat 2, measure 2, and *diminuendo* one dynamic level into staccato articulation in measure 3
4. *Mezzo forte* entrance of a solo line in the oboe and first cornet on count 4 of measure 3
5. Change to a more legato style in the motive played by clarinets and saxophones, measures 4 and 5.

MUSICAL EXAMPLE 1–3. **Howard Hanson, arranged by Erik W. G. Leidzen, March Carillion, beginning measures (condensed score).** Copyright 1940 by Theodore Presser Co. Used by permission.

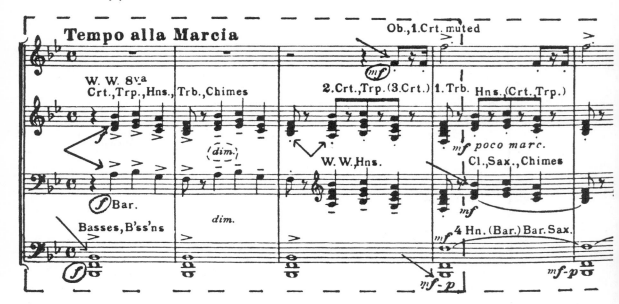

CONDUCTING PRACTICE

Once you have acquired familiarity with a score through musical analysis, conducting analysis, and hearing its overall sound, you are ready to practice conducting it. Conducting practice should be done as seriously as practice in any other performing medium. The main goal is to become confident of and comfortable with the various movements and gestures so that your concentration can remain primarily on the music (and ensemble) being conducted.

Practice Simulations

A basic problem in practicing conducting is the absence of the real instrument (an ensemble) during some stages of practice. One suggestion is to practice frequently with an imaginary choir, band, or orchestra before you. The purpose of this simulation is to keep in mind the relation between the voice lines and the physical location from which the sound is expected. It also trains you to establish eye contact with the imaginary soprano section, cello section, first oboist, or entire ensemble.

Practicing conducting a score without a live performing group often can be made more realistic and productive by supplying sound from another source. Obviously, a recorded performance of the work is one possibility. You can benefit from conducting with a recording, but keep in mind that the mechanically reproduced sound is unyielding and unresponsive to the "second conductor," who is more in the role of a follower than a leader.

Other ways of providing sound must be substituted if a recording is unavailable. One very useful tool in simulating sound is the vocalization of elements from the composite score in such a way as to provide a framework of the most important components to which a conductor must respond. These vocal sounds can take on various forms to meet the situation. In a choral score you can actually sing some of the parts, switching from one voice line to another as you conduct (this is also good ear training), or you might chant the words of the text in such a way as to capture important elements of the overall sound (such as attacks, entrances, dynamics, articulation, phrasing). Instrumental scores might be simulated more easily by vocalizing some of the musical happenings on a nonpitch syllable (such as *lah* or *tah*).

Figure 1–1 presents two applications of simulated practice with measures 7–11 of Musical Example 1–1, and Figure 1–2 shows use of a nonpitch syllable to vocalize sound from the score in Musical Example 1–3.

Practice Stages

Beginning conductors initially cannot practice all the techniques or attend every musical need that eventually will be applied in conducting a given score. You should attempt the task in stages, starting with the most basic factors and adding others as practice progresses. A three-stage model might serve as a general guide for accomplishing the objectives of practice:

FIGURE 1-1.   Practice Simulations for Musical Example 1–1 (measures 7–11)

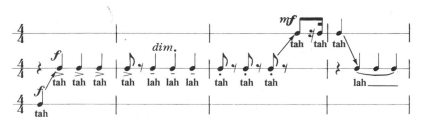

FIGURE 1-2.   Practice Simulation for Musical Example 1–3.

Stage 1. Set a steady and appropriate tempo in the beat pattern; apply the correct style (legato, marcato, staccato) to the beat; make adjustments to length and weight of the beat in accord with the fixed dynamics; clearly prepare for attacks of phrases.

Stage 2 (added to Stage 1). Give important cues, including those involving the left hand; make release gestures where needed; prepare other attacks in addition to the phrase attacks in Stage 1; adjust the beat to changes in tempo or dynamics.

Stage 3 (added to Stages 1 and 2). Communicate the shapes of phrases; attend to special effects or problems; respond to the piece as an entity—to its artistic wholeness.

MUSICAL TERMS

Musical terms and signs appear as part of the written score and provide additional information from the composer, arranger, or editor about how the music should be performed. Throughout the history of modern Western music (from the Renaissance to the present), composers have gradually included more and more markings in their scores. Renaissance composers supplied very little other than the notation itself, because their contemporaries knew the appropriate style and interpretation; any additional markings that appear in modern editions of this music have been put there by a music editor. The same is true to a lesser degree of music of the Baroque era. By the nineteenth century, composers explored a wider range of expressiveness in music and, accordingly, used more signs and terms. Most twentieth-century composers mark their scores carefully and in detail. Conductors have the responsibility of selecting music of composers, arrangers, or editors whose work they respect; it follows that they also have an obligation to perform the music as written and marked.

The following list includes more frequently encountered traditional terms, abbreviations, and signs used to communicate intended musical interpretation and style to the performer. (Terms referring to mechanics or techniques—*arco* and *con sordino*, for example—are not included.) You should memorize these terms in order to have instant recall of their meaning and application. In addition, you should have access to a dictionary of musical terms as a resource for finding the meanings of other markings encountered during the preparation of a musical score for conducting.

FIXED TEMPO

Very Slowest Tempo (M.M. 40–50)

Larghissimo	—superlative of *Largo*
Adagissimo	—superlative of *Adagio*
Lentissimo	—superlative of *Lento*

Very Slow Tempo (M.M. 50–63)

Largo	—broad, large
Adagio	—at ease
Lento	—slow

Slow Tempo (M.M. 63–72)

Larghetto	—diminutive of *Largo*
Adagietto	—diminutive of *Adagio*

Moderately Slow Tempo (M.M. 72–80)

Andante	–going or walking
Andantino	–diminutive of *Andante*, therefore meaning literally "going less"

Moderate Tempo (M.M. 80–92)

Moderato	–moderate

Moderately Rapid Tempo (M.M. 92–132)

Allegro	–cheerful, quick, lively
Allegretto	–diminutive of *Allegro;* a little slower

Very Rapid Tempo (M.M. 132–152)

con moto	–with motion
Vivo	–lively
Presto	–quick
Vivace	–vivacious
Presto assai	–very quick

Most Rapid Tempo Possible (M.M. 152–192)

Prestissimo	–superlative of *Presto*
Vivacissimo	–superlative of *Vivace*
Allegrissimo	–superlative of *Allegro*
Prestissimo possible	–extreme superlative of *Presto*

VARIABLE TEMPO

Gradual Increase of Tempo

Accelerando (accel.)	–hastening the movement
Stringendo (string.)	–quickening

Gradual Decrease of Tempo

Rallentando (rall.)	–gradually slower
Ritardando or *Ritenuto (rit.)*	–holding back

VARIABLE TEMPO AND LOUDNESS

Slower and Softer (gradually dying away)

Calando
Morendo
Perdendosi
Smorzando

Slower and Louder

Allargando

Louder and Faster

Crescendo ed animando

TEMPO QUALIFYING TERMS

assai	—very
ma non tanto	—but not too much
ma non troppo	—but not too much
meno mosso	—less quickly
molto	—very
non tanto	—not too much
non troppo	—not too much
piu mosso	—more quickly
poco	—little
poco a poco	—little by little

STABLE DYNAMICS

Softly as Possible

Pianississimo (ppp)
Pianissimo possible

Very Softly

Pianissimo (pp)
il pui piano
Piano assai

Softly

Piano (p)
piu piano

Moderately Softly

Mezzo Piano (mp)

Moderately Loudly

Mezzo Forte (mf)

Loudly

Forte (f)
piu forte

Very Loudly

Fortissimo (ff)
il piu forte

Loudly as Possible

Fortississimo (fff)
il piu forte possible

VARIABLE DYNAMICS

Accent of Single Note or Chord

Forzando or *Forzato (fz)*
Sforzando or *Sforzato (sf or sfz)*

Sudden Change

Forte– Piano (fp)	—loudly followed immediately by softly
Crescendo subito	—becoming louder immediately

More Gradual Change

Crescendo (cresc.)	—gradually becoming louder
Crescendo poco a poco	—becoming louder little by little
Crescendo molto	—becoming much louder
Crescendo poi diminuendo	—gradually louder then gradually
Crescendo e diminuendo	softer
Decrescendo (decresc.)	—gradually becoming softer
Diminuendo (dim.)	—gradually becoming softer

SPIRIT AND MOOD

Agitato	—excited, agitated
Animato	—with animation, lively
con amore	—with tenderness
con bravura	—with boldness
con energia	—with energy
con espressione; espressivo	—with expression; expressive
con brio	—with brilliance
con fucco	—with fire
con passione	—with passion
con grazia	—with grace
con tenerezza	—with tenderness
Dolce	—gently; sweetly
Giocoso	—humorously
Giojoso	—joyfully
Leggero; Leggiero	—light, rapid
Maestoso; con maesta	—majestically, dignified
Pastorale	—in pastoral style; simple, unaffected
Pesante	—heavy, weighty
Pomposo	—pompously
Scherzando; Scherzoso	—jokingly
Sostenuto	—sustained
Sotto voce	—with subdued voice

Physical Elements

You should recognize that physical factors are basic in building a technique on which you can develop as a skilled and artistic conductor. Proper base positions around which physical movement centers and the planes of movement through which the forms of conducting motion take place must be established as matters of good habit from the beginning of practice. Falling into bad habits of position or movement makes the task of becoming an effective conductor much more difficult because old habits must be broken and replaced with new ones before you can progress—usually a troublesome process.

Physical movement that is properly conceived and developed through practice leads toward conducting motions that are smoothly coordinated, well-timed, and clear. Such motions contribute to an acceptable appearance and assist the conductor in establishing himself as a leader of the ensemble. Moreover, they can be modified and extended in form to meet the full range of musical expression. We will now consider the factors that make up the correct base positions and the principles of movement on which conducting patterns are built.

BASE POSITIONS

Base positions in conducting can be thought of as stopped actions that capture basic elements within ongoing movement; they include posture, baton grip, and preparatory stance. The following analyses and photographs present models; you should frequently check your fundamental positions against these models while practicing.

Posture

The conductor's role is one of leadership. As a conductor your stance should reflect an attitude of confidence and a degree of aggressiveness; at the same time, it should allow you a full range of movement. Simply speaking, the basic stance is one of good posture: 1) erect but not stiff, 2) shoulders high, but free to move slightly forward, 3) chest high, not concave, 4) feet slightly apart with freedom to move either a half-step forward or backward, 5) weight distributed evenly on both feet, knees locked, and 6) head and eyes directed toward the ensemble.

Baton Grip

Every conductor should be able to conduct skillfully with a baton. The decision on whether or not to use a baton is eventually an individual—and sometimes arbitrary—one. Tradition among conductors seems to give credence to the conclusion that most instrumental conductors use a baton and most choral conductors do not, but separating fact from myth in the supporting rationale is difficult. Regardless of your ultimate decision, use of a baton while you are developing fundamental technique is strongly recommended because it can add an element of discipline to the conducting movements. Practicing basic patterns of movement separately in both the right and left hand with a baton can help developing controlled motion in each hand, but other than for this type of practice you should always conduct with the baton in your right hand, whether you are naturally right- or left-handed.

Two of the most acceptable grips of the right hand are shown in Figure 2–1. (Grips in the left hand would be the same except for the normal mirror effect on left–right direction.) For the present you should use only one grip in holding a baton and practice consistently with that method. Your ultimate choice of grips will be determined by personal preference, which might be either grip *a*, grip *b*, shifting from one to the other, or a grip that is different from either of those pictured.

Grip *a* has these characteristics: (1) The butt of the baton is brought into contact with the palm of the hand for stability. (2) A three-finger contact is created on the shaft of the baton. The primary grip is between the cushion of the thumb and the first joint of the middle finger, with the index finger resting lightly but

FIGURE 2–1. Baton Grips   **A**   **B**

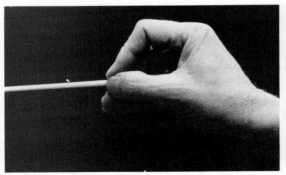
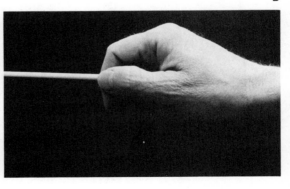

firmly on top of the shaft above the primary grip. (3) The fourth and fifth fingers are separated slightly from those that contact the baton. (4) The hand assumes a natural, relaxed, arched shape with the palm relatively parallel to the floor. Some persons prefer this grip because the baton feels like a natural extension of the hand and forearm, while the sense of focus for movement remains more in the hand than in the stick.

Grip b for holding a baton differs from A because the primary grip on the shaft is between the cushion of the thumb and the first joint of the index finger, with the remaining fingers closed around the butt. Some persons prefer this grip because it provides a feel of firmness and physical control over the baton and because they sense a projection of the conducting motion into its tip.

Preparatory (home-base) Position

The so-called preparatory position functions in two ways. First, it is the stance taken by a conductor prior to giving the initial attack at the beginning of a piece of music; it is the attention, or ready, attitude. Second, the preparatory position serves as a home-base reference point from which well-formed movement in any direction can be made—a point to range from and return to. Incorrect positioning of arm, hand, and baton probably will carry over into the conducting movement and limit its effectiveness. Acquiring a good preparatory position as a matter of habit should be one of your primary objectives.

Figure 2–2 shows both a front and side view of a correct preparatory stance and home-base position. Study the next analysis of various components of this stance and, at the same time, compare them with incorrect positions pictured in Figure 2–3.

Elbow. The elbow is one of the main keys to proper arm position and motion in conducting. It should be one loose hand's width away from the side of the body and at, or slightly ahead of, a vertical line that would bisect the torso (Figure 2–2).

FIGURE 2–2. Correct Preparatory Position   **A**   **B**

A

B

C

D

FIGURE 2-3. Incorrect Preparatory Positions

In Figure 2-3, pose A shows the elbow held too tightly against the body, B shows it held high and far to the outside, C shows the elbow retracted and the hand and baton pulled too close to the front of the body, and A shows the elbow, arm, and baton extended too far forward. Starting from any of the home-base positions in Figure 2-3 would result in ongoing patterns of movement that are restricted in some fundamental way (for example, tense, awkward, too large or too small, too far from or too close to the body).

Forearm. Figure 2–2 shows the forearm extending forward and slightly inward, in a plane essentially parallel to the floor. Movement from this position would keep the hand and baton in good location relative to the torso and head. Figure 2–3 B and D present a situation in which the forearm and upper arm are more in the form of one straight unit reaching or stretching away from the body. Movement from this position would be primarily from the shoulder in a stiff-arm style.

Upper Arm. Given good posture and proper location of the elbow, the upper arm will also be in an acceptable position, because it takes its only possible place between elbow and shoulder. Therefore, concentration on positioning elbow, forearm, and hand will give excellent form to the entire arm and avoid some of the extremes represented in Figure 2–3.

Hand and Wrist. The hand is a natural extension of the forearm and should appear as such. This means that the wrist (a movable joint) should remain firm enough in the base positions to keep the hand from creating a severe angle with the forearm by tilting down or up, or breaking to the inside or outside. Flexibility and movement in the wrist becomes involved in the context of ongoing gestures and beat patterns. Observe also in Figures 2–1 and 2–2 that the hand and fingers have an arched shape and the palm is more or less parallel to the floor. When you are conducting without a baton, the hand retains a similar shape. Merely remove the baton and loosen the fingers so they do not still appear to be gripping something.

MOVEMENT IN CONDUCTING

A conductor's main function is to communicate through movement with the singers or players during rehearsal and public performance. Most of this movement comes from the arm and hand. Arm motion travels various geometric routes and is a result of coordinated movement at the joints of the shoulder, elbow, wrist, and fingers. Understanding the principles of controlled movement and learning to apply these principles through practice can help you establish good basic habits in your conducting patterns.

Planes of Movement

Imagine the home-base preparatory position of the hand as a starting point. Movement of the hand from this point will follow, to some degree, the vertical and lateral (horizontal) axes that intersect it. Whether the lines are essentially straight or curved, the hand (and baton) can move upward and downward or outward and inward.

Vertical plane. Figure 2–4 shows correct positions at the top and bottom points of the vertical plane of motion. An imaginary line of hand movement drawn from top to bottom, or bottom to top, will trace a relatively straight line that goes through the home-base position. Compare this with the route of hand movement in Figure 2–5; in the latter case the path would be more in the form of an arc that loops backward at both the top and bottom. Greater clarity of beat and control of a

FIGURE 2–4.   Correct Vertical Plane of Movement

FIGURE 2-5.   Incorrect Vertical Plane of Movement

range of musical effects (soft, loud, smooth, accented) are possible with vertical movements that follow a straighter line and shorter distance.

Lateral plane. Movement from side to side of the home-base hand position can be thought of as direction (right–left) or in relation to the body (outside–inside). Outside is to the right in the right hand but to the left in the left hand. Observe in Figure 2–6 that a line between the outside and inside positions of the hand is again relatively straight. Each side position is about equidistant to the right or left of home base and at a similar distance in front of the body. This form of lateral motion can be controlled over a wide range of force (light to heavy) and over various lengths from six to thirty or more inches. It also remains highly visible to all persons in the ensemble.

Figure 2–7 pictures excessive lateral movement. A line tracing the hand from

A

B

FIGURE 2–6. Correct Lateral Plane of Movement

FIGURE 2–7. Incorrect Lateral Plane of Movement

A

B

right to left, or left to right, would form a large arc of wasted motion and show loss of control at the extreme points.

Movement at the Joints

All primary movement in the conductor's beat pattern starts from three movable joints—shoulder, elbow, and wrist. How, and to what extent, movement in these joints is employed determines the effectiveness and appearance of the beat. Excess flexibility in the joints results in vague, floppy gestures, whereas too much rigidity contributes to tense, jerky motions. The following principles governing movement at the elbow, shoulder, and wrist are important and basic to disciplined, expressive, and coordinated conducting. They also summarize what can be seen by continued viewing of the preceding photographs.

Elbow. The elbow joint is the only one of the three from which movement always occurs in conducting, for this is the only way the forearm, hand, and baton can move in space. With very little or no movement from the shoulder and upper arm, the forearm (plus hand and baton) can go in any of the four possible directions—down, up, outward, or inward. It can trace vertical, horizontal, or circular (curved) lines in the air. Most of the basic moderate movement in conducting comes from the elbow through the forearm and wrist.

Shoulder. When musical events in a score require an increased range in the scope (size) of conducting gestures, the movable shoulder joint and, consequently, the upper arm become more involved. Upward motion that extends the hand and baton to head level or above pulls the entire arm movement from the shoulder until the elbow is forward and the upper arm is approximately parallel—and the forearm diagonal—to the floor (Figure 2–4A). A gesture that fully extends the hand and baton to the outside will pull the elbow farther away from the side of the body than its home-base point, and the upper arm will establish a greater angle with the vertical plane of the body (Figure 2–6A).

Increased movement from the shoulder joint must be accompanied by corresponding movement at the elbow and wrist. Movement only at the shoulder indicates that the elbow and wrist are locked, that the entire arm moves as a rigid unit. The result is an awkward, tense, clublike gesture.

Wrist. The wrist joint is another important physiological element in effective conducting. It allows the hand to make either vertical or lateral movement in relation to the position of the forearm of which it is an extension. However, movement from the wrist alone should never be employed; we cannot conduct effectively with hand motion only.

The appearance and expressive effect of the hand and baton at points in the conductor's patterns where the forearm changes direction (down to up, or, left to right, for example) is influenced by whether the wrist is locked or flexible. A flexible wrist is part of the hand's follow-through to the arm's movement. The wrist is involved in conducting motions in three primary ways: (1) The wrist should be slightly elastic in a smooth legato beat, permitting the hand to float easily and cushion the points of directional change. Wrist movement should never be so loose that the hand becomes floppy. (2) A sharper movement from the wrist is required in making a staccato beat, so that the hand and baton will have more snap at the points of the beats. (3) A virtually locked wrist is necessary in a marcato (accented) beat, so that appropriate force can be generated from the arm into the hand and baton.

Hand. The shape of the hand, the way it grips a baton, and its base positions in conjunction with the arm have been pictured and discussed. It has also been mentioned that the palm should be down (parallel to the floor) in the preparatory position and during vertical and lateral movement. You should avoid a hand position in which the palm faces inward most of the time because this results in vertical movement led by the side of the hand in a chopping, cutting motion and lateral movement led inside by the palm and outside by the back of the hand— generally weak motions. At the same time, you must realize that on occasion it is good to vary the form of movement. A slight rotation of the hand at points of lateral changes in direction might contribute to the flow of a legato beat, but too much turning of the hand will tend to blur the line of movement. Crossing from inside to outside with the palm leading can be used to communicate unusual force, such as a hard accent, whereas, the same motion done as a backhand gesture could suggest a pulling or stretching of sound. But for now, stay with the basic principle —palm down.

PRACTICE ACTIVITIES

1. Stand before a mirror and take a preparatory stance with the right hand holding a baton. Check positions of your elbow, forearm, hand, and baton with reference to Figure 2–2 and related points discussed in the text. Repeat the preparatory position with the left hand (alone) holding the baton, and again with both hands at the same time (baton in the right hand). Practice these positions until you can assume them comfortably and automatically.

2. Practice movement in the vertical plane, starting from the home-base position and striving to keep a relatively straight line of motion from top to bottom (Figure 2–4). Keep the wrist flexible at the points of change in direction. Practice in front of and away from a mirror in the following ways:
   a. right hand, without baton, beginning with a twelve-inch-long motion and gradually increasing the length until the arm reaches its normal full extension above the head and below the waist
   b. left hand, without baton, in a similar manner
   c. both hands in a similar manner
   d. both hands, with baton in the right.

3. Practice movement in the lateral plane, starting from home-base position and striving to keep a relatively straight line from side to side (Figure 2–6). Allow the wrist to flex sideways at the points of change in direction. Practice without and with a baton in the following ways:
   a. right hand alone, gradually increasing the length of stroke until there is a normal full extension to the inside and outside

    b. left hand alone in a similar manner

    c. both hands at the same time. (The hands will go in opposite right–left directions, moving toward and away from each other but never overlapping.)

4. Combine movement in the vertical and lateral planes, with one hand moving in each plane, in order to begin achieving left-hand independence from the right. Practice in the following ways:

    a. Beginning with each hand at preparatory home-base, simultaneously start the right hand moving up and the left hand moving in and continue the vertical up-down motion of the right hand coordinated with the in-out motion of the left.

    b. Reverse the planes so that vertical movement is in the left hand and lateral movement in the right.

5. Change the straight lateral line to a more curved motion. Begin at home-base (each hand separately, then together), and move from side to side in a figure-eight form, starting in a downward-inward direction.

THREE

The Three-Beat Pattern

Chapters Three, Four, and Five present many of the basic techniques you will need as a conductor and apply them to conducting in a three-beat pattern. By the time you have acquired these skills, you will be ready and able to conduct some complete pieces, or major sections, in triple meter. The three-beat pattern is introduced first because it involves both vertical and lateral planes and because it is one of the easiest patterns in which to make coordinated, well-formed movement. Going on to other beat patterns and additional techniques presented in subsequent chapters becomes a relatively easy task.

In this chapter you will learn to develop a properly executed three-beat pattern and to apply it in sizes appropriate to a range of dynamic levels and in different styles of musical articulation. Chapter Four will give you an opportunity to gain skills in controlling attacks of various kinds, in cueing voice parts in either hand, and in communicating expressive values in the music. Chapter Five will treat different types of releases and special situations created by fermatas.

INTERPRETATION OF METER

The conductor's beat pattern is always based on the number of pulsations, or beats, actually felt per measure (that is, beats that can be maintained as governors and regulators of ongoing patterns of rhythm in the music). You must make three initial decisions with regard to conducting any score: What kind of note functions as the beat unit (receiving one beat's duration); how many beats are there per complete measure; and which pattern of movement is appropriate to the meter and number of beats per measure?

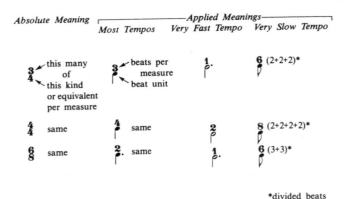

FIGURE 3–1. Model for Interpreting Meter Signatures

Determination of the beat unit and the resulting number of beats involves interpretation of the meter (time) signature for a given score. Any meter signature can have two accurate meanings, which we will call its *absolute* meaning and its *applied* meaning. Absolute meaning is the one that is always true; applied meaning is an actual indicator of the kind of note that should function as the beat unit and, consequently, governs the number of felt beats in each measure. A given meter signature has only one absolute meaning, but most have two or three practical applied meanings. The applied meaning most appropriate to a specific piece of music is derived from musical factors such as tempo, style, tradition, type of ensemble, and performance conditions. Tempo is the strongest determinant of applied meaning, as illustrated in Figure 3–1, which shows absolute and applied meanings of three common signatures.

Figure 3–2 shows meter signatures and corresponding applied meanings for which you would conclude that a three-beat pattern should be used.

FIGURE 3–2. Applicable Meters for a Three-Beat Pattern

Simple Meters

$\frac{3}{4}$ applied as 3♩

$\frac{3}{8}$ applied as 3♪

$\frac{3}{2}$ applied as 3♩

Compound Meters

$\frac{9}{8}$ applied as 3♩.

$\frac{9}{4}$ applied as 3♩.

FORM OF THE BEAT PATTERN

Components of a Beat's Form

Knowledge of the basic form of a conducting beat, along with terms that refer to its component parts, is a useful prerequisite to the study and application of complete beat patterns. Figure 3–3 gives you a graphic representation of the first two beats of a three-beat pattern, with parts labeled. Definitions follow.

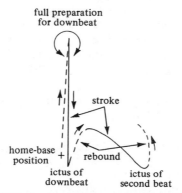

FIGURE 3–3. Components of a Beat's Form

Ictus. An ictus is the exact point in time when the tempo beat occurs. It corresponds to the click of a metronome and marks the beginning of a beat's duration, but itself has no literal duration. (*Tempo beat* refers to the rhythmic beat, or pulse, at the ongoing tempo.) Every ictus is approached in a certain direction along the vertical and lateral planes of movement in the conductor's pattern (for example, down, outside).

Stroke. The portion of the motion that leads in the direction of, and ends in, an ictus is called a stroke (solid lines in Figure 3–3). Some degree of downward direction is always involved in the stroke into any ictus. In Figure 3–3, for example, the stroke of beat 1 is straight down, and that of beat 2 leads downward as well as to the outside.

Rebound. Motion from any ictus must continue with a rebound (sometimes called a recoil) from that point. The rebound is in a general opposite direction to the stroke into the preceding ictus and continues into the stroke for the next ictus. Figure 3–3 depicts a rebound from the downbeat ictus starting upward, then leading to the stroke down and out into the ictus of beat 2. Change of direction from stroke to rebound is what sets off the exact point of an ictus.

Preparation. Movement following an ictus, or starting from the home-base position, functions as preparation for the next ictus or beat. We will use the term *full preparation* in reference to this complete motion (including rebound and stroke components) between consecutive ictus points, or between the preparatory (home-base) position and the downbeat ictus (Figure 3–3). Indeed, movement that occurs between ictus points is the most important part of the form of a beat pattern, for it is this motion that provides cues to the exact moment of the next ictus, to the ongoing tempo and style, and to the level of loudness.

Downbeat. Every metrical beat pattern (for example, triple, duple) in conducting starts with a downbeat; every bar line should be crossed with a downbeat. Preparation for an initial downbeat (Figure 3–3) begins from near the home-base position, which can be thought of as an imaginary ictus for the preceding beat— the last beat of the preceding measure. Full preparation (sometimes called the preparatory beat) for an attack on the downbeat is a continuous motion comprised of an upward rebound and a reversal into a downward stroke ending in the ictus. Upward and downward movement is essentially in the same vertical plane, although the broken-line upward direction in Figure 3–3 is offset slightly so that it is visible. A preparatory beat should set the tempo, style, and dynamic level of the ongoing music.

Practice exercises. Practice preparatory beats for a downbeat, including its rebound, in the following ways:

1. Right hand alone with baton
   a. moderate tempo, moderately loud
   b. moderate tempo, loud
   c. moderate tempo, soft
   d. slow tempo, soft
   e. slow tempo, loud
   f. fast tempo, moderately loud.
2. Repeat exercise 1 using left hand alone with baton.
3. Repeat exercise 1 using both hands together, baton in the right hand.

Three-Beat Form

Figure 3–4 displays the basic three-beat pattern of movement for the right hand and its mirror image in the left hand. Refer to these drawings while you study the verbal descriptions related to them.

FIGURE 3–4. Three-Beat Pattern

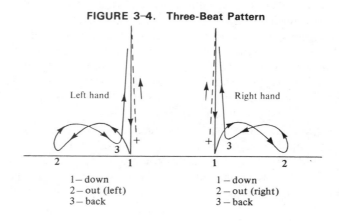

Left hand	Right hand
1 – down	1 – down
2 – out (left)	2 – out (right)
3 – back	3 – back

Direction. Directions of the three beats in relation to the body position are the same for each hand—down, out, and back. Beat 1 should have a stroke that is straight down into the ictus, rather than one that slants or slides to either side. Beat 2 moves outside from the rebound in a right and downward direction in the right hand and left and downward in the left hand. "Back" is a better description than "up" for what actually happens in the form of the final beat, because it refers to an ictus point that is near home base and in the vicinity of the ictus of beat 1. Such a motion on the last beat of any meter results in a stroke moving slightly downward into an ictus at a point from which a full rebound can be made as part of the preparation for the next downbeat. Stroking upward into an ictus invariably results in a weak motion. You should remember to keep the palm of your hand facing essentially downward throughout the entire pattern of movement.

Ictus points. A clear ictus should be established at the point of each beat. Clarity is the result of a clean stroke into the ictus and an appropriate rebound from it. The downbeat should hit an imaginary "base line," which might be lower or higher than the home-base preparatory position, depending on the relative size of the complete pattern. Ictus points for beats 2 and 3 are normally slightly above the base line; however, this situation will vary with special musical events (such as accents) that might occur on these beats.

Rebounds. Every ictus should be followed by a rebound that has a clear direction (usually opposite that of the stroke) and an appropriate size and style in relation to the overall beat pattern. In general, the length of the rebound should not be more than half the length of the stroke; it is often less.

Right and left hand. Your right hand always has the primary responsibility for maintaining the ongoing beat pattern, whether or not you are naturally right-handed. It is also the hand that holds the baton whenever one is used. Beat patterns of the correct form and of various sizes and styles must be practiced in the right hand until they occur automatically in response to thinking about the musical score instead of the beat pattern *per se*.

Generally, the left hand should not be used in conjunction with the right to conduct the beat pattern measure after measure. It has important special roles to be introduced later. Even so, practicing basic beat patterns with the left hand can aid in developing coordinated movement that will enable you to adapt more readily to independent left-hand gestures. You should be able to make any movement with the left hand you can make with the right, and make it equally well.

Practice exercises. Practice the basic three-beat pattern for a period of eight measures in the following ways. Repeat each way until the movement feels coordinated and comfortable, and until the form of the pattern presents a good appearance (view yourself in a mirror).

1. Right hand alone (with baton, then without)
2. Left hand alone (with baton, then without)
3. Both hands together (baton in right hand).

SIZE OF THE BEAT PATTERN

The wide ranges of aesthetic content in music require continuous modifications in the beat pattern in order for the conductor to communicate correct effects and appear in harmony with them. The beat pattern cannot be repeated measure after measure in exactly the same way. A good maxim might be: "The conductor should look like the music sounds."

One of the necessary changes to meet variations in musical demands takes place in the size and scope of movements. Discussion of basic principles involved in the size of beat patterns requires consideration of three factors: points of reference, variable elements, and musical determinants. Figure 3–5 illustrates the comments in the next sections.

Points of Reference

Size of a beat pattern could be defined in inches: a twenty-four-inch movement is large in comparison with a six-inch one. However, a twenty-four-inch movement that appears appropriate when executed by a conductor whose height is six feet, six inches will appear larger and out of proportion when made by one who is only five feet, two inches. A better way to gauge size of pattern is in relation to the individual making the movement. The forehead, shoulder, and belt levels are good points of reference for size in the vertical plane. Size of movement to the outside is sensed by the degree to which the arm is extended away from the torso. However, no distinction in size of the beat (or in any other factor of conducting) should be made on the basis of whether the conductor is male or female. Both men and women should approach basic conducting in the same way, and their conducting patterns should take on similar form and appearance.

Length and Weight

Two physical elements that alter size and scope in a conductor's beat pattern are the length and weight of motions. *Length* of a beat is involved in both the stroke into an ictus and the rebound from it. Perception of distance should be gauged between positions of the hand rather than with reference to the tip of the

FIGURE 3–5. Comparative Sizes of a Beat Pattern

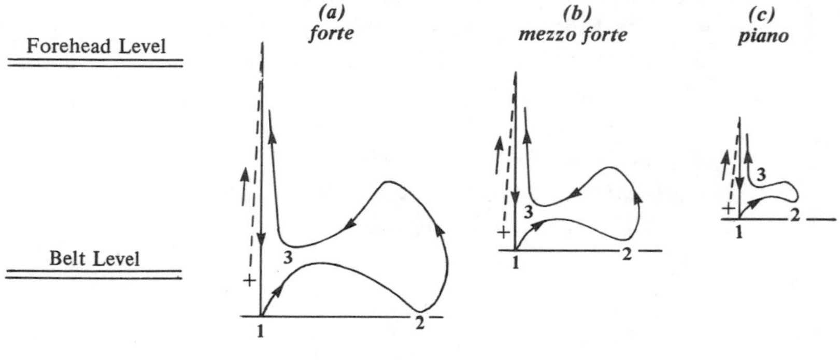

baton. A long downstroke might move from a hand position slightly above the forehead to below belt level (Figure 3–5a). The baton tip would be higher than the hand at the top of the stroke and lower at the bottom. In comparison, a short downstroke might cover a distance from slightly below the collarbone to the lower part of the rib cage. Rebounds from longer strokes are usually proportionally longer than those from shorter strokes.

The *weight* of movement refers to the relative amount of muscular force involved, ranging from light to heavy. Weight is sometimes disproportionate to length. Whereas a long stroke is often heavier, a shorter stroke also can be made in a forceful manner. Heavy beats should never create the type of muscular tension that results in a rigid, restricted motion. On the other hand, a light beat should not be so relaxed that it becomes lifeless. Some degree of muscular resilience should exist in all conducting movement.

Musical Determinants

Relative size of a beat pattern that is appropriate to a given musical passage is determined primarily by loudness and tempo. Loudness levels (often called dynamics) are reflected in both the length and weight of the beat pattern. Other things being equal, *forte* passages are conducted by using longer and heavier movements; *piano* sections require shorter, lighter motions (Figure 3–5).

Tempo is another determinant of length and weight. Length of strokes and rebounds in a *forte* passage at a quick tempo must be shortened, but the element of weight can be retained or increased. At a *piano* level in slow tempo, duration between ictus points must still be filled with movement, and this might require a slight increase in length of beat compared with a similar passage at a moderately fast tempo.

Musical Examples 3–1 and 3–2 quote two familiar instrumental themes that illustrate contrasting levels of loudness, tempos, and conducting movements. Practice conducting each while thinking or singing the melody. Example 3–1 requires a large, heavy three-beat pattern at a moderately slow tempo. Example 3–2 must be conducted with a small, light beat at a quick tempo.

MUSICAL EXAMPLE 3–1. **Tchaikovsky, Symphony No. 4 in F Minor, Movement I, beginning measures.**

MUSICAL EXAMPLE 3–2. **Tchaikovsky, Symphony No. 5 in E Minor, Movement III, beginning measures.**

STYLE OF THE BEAT PATTERN

Style, as an element of the beat pattern, relates primarily to the type of articulation of sounds called for in the music. It may also have some connection with the general mood of the music (and the text in choral music). The two basic styles are legato and marcato-staccato, with various gradations and modifications of each. Conducting motions must communicate to the singers or players the appropriate style of articulation as well as the metrical tempo beat and dynamic level. Conducting in one style while the music is sounding in another produces a frustrating aural-visual dissonance. Study and compare the styles of a three-beat pattern displayed in Figure 3–6 and their characteristics as described in the text.

Normal Legato (Figure 3–6b)

Movement between ictus points is in a continuous, smoothly flowing motion that should start with the initial preparatory beat. Speed of the motion remains essentially the same throughout its duration between ictus points. Form of the motion is more curved—except for the downstroke—than the marcato-staccato style.

Ictus points are clear, but they provide a softer cushion between stroke and rebound than found in the marcato-staccato style, and they are less rounded than the style of extreme legato. The wrist should be slightly flexible, especially at points where there is a change in direction.

Extreme Legato (Figure 3–6a)

Some passages in music require a more flowing and connected style than experienced in normal legato articulation. Reference to this extreme style can be expressed in terms such as *expressivo legato* or *molto legato*. The ictus in *expressivo-legato* style is curved; stroke and rebound are connected in a continuous curving motion.

Expressivo-legato beats should be used sparingly. Continuing this style over long periods increases the possibility that the singers or players may lose their feeling for exact timing of the beat points.

FIGURE 3–6. Comparative Styles of a Beat Pattern

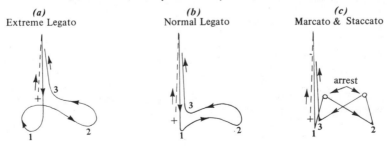

(a)	*(b)*	*(c)*
Extreme Legato	Normal Legato	Marcato & Staccato

Marcato (Figure 3–6c)

Strokes in marcato style have relatively heavy weight moving into an ictus. For this reason, the wrist is kept locked so the force of the arm can be employed effectively. Ictus points are heavier and well marked by a more angular rebound.

Movement between ictus points is characterized by an arrest (stop)—represented by a small circle in Figure 3–6—which occurs at the top of each rebound and before the following stroke. Due to the arrest of motion, the stroke picks up speed moving into the ictus so that the point of the beat will arrive at its exact moment.

Marcato patterns follow straighter lines and more severe angles than legato patterns do.

Staccato (Figure 3–6c)

A staccato beat pattern has many of the characteristics of marcato style, including arrests, straight strokes, and sharp rebounds. Staccato beats usually are lighter in weight and shorter in length than those in marcato style. They also require more wrist activity in the form of a snap or slap (not to be overdone) at ictus points.

During your analysis of the music you must decide which style of beat is appropriate in each phrase, in each measure, and sometimes on each note. Differentiation in style is relatively easy among light staccato, marcato, normal legato, and extreme legato articulations. Heavy (*forte, fortissimo*) staccato, however, is conducted essentially the same as marcato. Signs in the score for legato (slur), accent, or staccato provide clear indications for articulation. When markings are absent, you must first determine how the passage should be played or sung, then conduct it in the corresponding style.

The lyrical melody in Musical Example 3–3 has an intrinsic feel of legato, as well as slur markings in the score. Although accompanying parts (not shown) are in softly syncopated semistaccato patterns, the conductor would give primary attention to and conduct in the style of the melodic theme.

Markings in the score in Musical Example 3–4 give directions to perform it "with fire" and at a *forte* level. A marcato style of articulation for both the chorus and conductor is required to capture this spirit of the music and text.

MUSICAL EXAMPLE 3–3. **Schubert, Symphony in B Minor (Unfinished), Movement I, measures 44–53 (Cello).**

MUSICAL EXAMPLE 3–4.   **Mendelssohn, Elijah, No. 20, Thanks be to God, beginning measures (Chorus).**

NONPITCH PRACTICE EXERCISES

Conduct the following nonpitch exercises, which have musical elements of rhythm, dynamics, phrasing, and articulation. Nonpitch exercises provide good practice material because they can include all of the elements for which you need to develop conducting skills (of course, pitch per se cannot be communicated), and because the sounds can be easily vocalized (with such sounds as, *tah, lah, too, loo, tee*).

1. Conduct both phrases in legato style and at the tempo and dynamic level indicated.

2. Change the size of your beat during the preparatory motion for the downbeat of measure 5 to signal the soft attack, and continue through the second phrase at a *piano* level without any change in tempo or style.

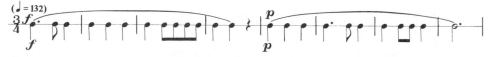

3. Your full preparation (preparatory beat) for the initial attack should incorporate a feel for the tempo, *forte* dynamic, and marcato style of the first phrase. Change to *mezzo piano* and staccato style through the second phrase, and introduce more snap in your wrist motion for the staccato beat. Eighth notes followed by eighth rests are articulated in essentially the same way as staccato quarter notes.

4. Change your beat style between legato and staccato as marked. Keep tempo and dynamics the same throughout.

Musical examples for study and practice. Conducting excerpts from music scores requires a thorough familiarity with the sound of the music so that the feel you have for all of its elements can be transferred to your physical movements as a natural response. Play or sing the excerpts, as necessary, to acquire an aural concept of the music.

1. Practice conducting previously quoted Musical Examples 3–1, 3–2, 3–3, and 3–4 using beat patterns of appropriate size and style to communicate the music's tempo, dynamic level, and articulation.

2. The oboe solo in Musical Example 3–5 flows gracefully at a moderately quick tempo in a basically legato style. Accents on count 3 and slurred staccato notes (semistaccato) are moderate articulations of their kinds. Start with a light, normal legato beat and add a small amount of wrist snap through measures 5–7.

MUSICAL EXAMPLE 3–5. **Brahms, Symphony No. 2 in D Major, Movement III, beginning measures (Oboe 1).**

3. Start the next excerpt for mixed chorus with a normal legato beat at the tempo indicated. Try shifting to a more *expressivo-legato* style (Figure 3–6) in the second and third measures.

MUSICAL EXAMPLE 3–6. **Schubert, Mass in G Major, Kyrie, beginning measures (Chorus).**

4. *Forte* staccato phrases in Musical Example 3–7 can be conducted with a marcato beat in which the strokes are of moderate length (because of the quick tempo) and heavy weight. Change to a soft attack and legato style with count 3,

measure 8. Measures 9–16 provide an excellent challenge to your ability to shift from legato to staccato and back exactly as marked in the score. Repeated practice will be necessary.

MUSICAL EXAMPLE 3–7.   **Mozart, Symphony No. 39 in E Flat Major, Movement III, beginning measures (Violin 1).**

On-Beat Attacks

The ability to communicate precise attacks is one of the most important basic skills for a conductor to acquire. Attacks can be classified into two general categories—*on-beat* and *after-beat*. On-beat attacks are those in which the sound starts at the beginning of a beat's duration, or at the ictus. After-beat attacks happen at some point within a beat's duration, following the ictus, and will be dealt with in a later chapter. Important places in a score where the conductor needs to prepare for attacks in one or more voice lines include those that start a phrase and those within a phrase where musical effects of a special nature occur. We will refer to the two kinds of situations as *on-beat phrase attacks* and *internal on-beat attacks*. When skill in preparing for important attacks is added to other techniques developed in chapter three, it will be possible to turn our attention at the end of this chapter to conducting for expressive performance of phrase lines.

ON-BEAT PHRASE ATTACKS

Phrase attacks can occur on any beat of a measure, therefore at any ictus of a conducting pattern. Three-beat patterns include possible attacks on the downbeat, on beat 2 to the outside, and on beat 3 near home-base position. *Phrase attack* refers to the start of the initial tone of a phrase. Although communication of good phrase attacks throughout a piece is important, the opening phrase and entrances of voice parts during the course of the music are points that require particularly effective attacks.

Right-Hand Preparations

Every attack must be prepared. On-beat attacks require a full preparatory motion that is equivalent to the preceding rebound and stroke. The preparation starts moving in a continuous motion away from then back to the ictus of the attack beat, moves into the attack ictus with a degree of downward direction in the stroke (along with any right or left direction involved), and leads to a clear ictus for the point of attack.

Full preparation for attacks on the downbeat was presented in chapter three and needs no further explanation here. Study the graphic representations of preparations for attacks on beats 2 and 3 in Figure 4–1 along with a summary of their characteristics in the text.

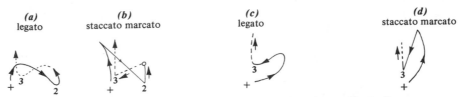

| (a) | (b) | (c) | (d) |
| legato | staccato marcato | legato | staccato marcato |

FIGURE 4–1. Preparatory Motions for Attacks on Beats 2 and 3 of a Three-Beat Pattern

Attacks on beat 2. Beat 2 of a three-beat pattern is to the outside. Figure 4–1 shows full preparations that would apply for any on-beat attack to the outside (such as, beat 2 of a three-beat pattern, beat 3 of a four-beat pattern). The starting point is at or near the ictus of beat 1—the preceding beat—and the full preparatory movement fills the duration between ictus points of beats 1 and 2. A rebound completes the attack ictus and would lead into the stroke for the next beat. The exact form, size, and style of the preparatory motion must be in accord with the dynamic level, tempo, and articulation of the music. Compare legato and staccato-marcato forms in Figure 4–1.

Attacks on beat 3. The ictus for the final beat of any pattern is back to the vicinity of the downbeat (or home-base position). Therefore, full preparation for an on-beat attack on beat 3 of a three-beat pattern is the same as for the last beat of other patterns. Figure 4–1 depicts preparatory motions starting from home-base position, moving out and up, then stroking down and into the attack ictus on beat 3, and rebounding to cross the bar line into the next downbeat. Compare the legato and staccato-marcato forms and you can see that the latter provides for either more force in loud marcato attacks or for more crispness in light staccato attacks.

Conducting Phrase Attacks

Initial attacks on the first phrase of a piece, or at the beginning of a movement, start from the preparatory stance with the preparatory beat given in a form that will signal attack on the correct beat of the measure. Timing is extremely important. If the preparatory movement starts too soon or too late, some or all of the singers or players will attack before or after the ictus. You can check your timing (for practice only) by counting out one complete measure to set your feeling of the tempo; then in the second measure start the preparatory motion, immediately following an imaginary ictus on the count preceding the attack, and arrive precisely at the attack ictus on the next count. Always be sure to use an acceptable form of preparatory motion (Figure 4–1); any extra movement or change of direction will spoil the timing.

Attacks on some of the subsequent phrases throughout the piece may require no special attention from the conductor. Players and singers can be expected to phrase, take a breath as necessary, and attack in context with the ongoing music and conducting pattern. In other situations, especially with relatively inexperienced ensembles, effective and precise phrasing rests largely in the hands of the conductor. Artistic phrasing results from both the sense of punctuation at the end of one phrase and a clear attack to start the next. Conductors of choral ensembles are more frequently apt to be attentive to phrasing and phrase attacks because of the strong alliance between structure and meaning in the text and phrase design in the music. Phrasing technique in conducting ordinarily involves relaxing the beat—making it smaller and lighter—at the cadence of the preceding phrase and relatively increasing the size of the preparatory motion leading to the next phrase attack. In this way the beat becomes more visible to the singers or players and, at the same time, creates a psychological impulse on their part to respond to the phrase punctuation and attack. In phrases where the cadence is a point of climax and stress, the beat must retain vigor, size, and weight, but the preparatory motion for the next phrase attack can still be clearly identified. Figure 4–2 presents some instances where the conductor should differentiate the cadence of one phrase and attack of the next. You should practice conducting each example.

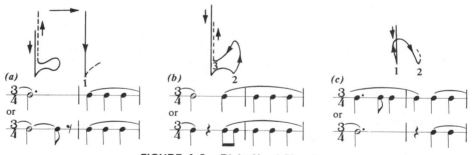

FIGURE 4–2. Right-Hand Phrasings

Musical examples for study and practice. The following musical excerpts will give you opportunities to practice preparations for initial attacks and subsequent phrasing attacks. Learn the music, select an appropriate form of preparation for the initial attack (Figure 4–1) and for the next phrase attack (Figure 4–2), and then conduct the excerpt several times while thinking or singing the melody.

1. Prepare for the initial attack on a downbeat in legato style and at a soft dynamic and slow tempo. Conduct phrases of two, two, and three measures in length, employing a phrase-attack motion like that shown in Figure 4–2a at points where the music phrases off of the dotted-half notes and starts a new phrase on the next downbeat.

MUSICAL EXAMPLE 4–1. **Bach, Come, Soothing Death (Komm, Süsser Tod), beginning measures.**

2. In Musical Example 4–2, use the marcato form of preparation shown in Figure 4–1 for the initial *forte* attack on beat 3, and apply form *b* from Figure 4–2 in measure 4 where the quarter rest separates the cadence of phrase one and the attack of phrase two. Your downbeat on the cadence note should remain at a *forte* level. This should be followed by a very small stroke into a light ictus on the rest (beat 2) and a relatively enlarged preparatory motion moving to the ictus of beat 3 where the second phrase starts *piano* and legato.

MUSICAL EXAMPLE 4–2. **Haydn, Symphony No. 101 in D Major (Clock), Movement III, beginning measures (Violin 1).**

3. The twelve-measure theme in Musical Example 4–3 opens with two-measure motives followed by eight measures of unpunctuated melody. Apply form *b*, Figure 4–2, in measures 2 and 4 by relaxing and decreasing the motion on beat 2, then enlarging the preparatory motion into beat 3. You will feel this response as an intrinsic part of the music if you give sound to the melody as you practice conducting it.

MUSICAL EXAMPLE 4–3. **Brahms, Symphony No. 3 in F Major, Movement III, beginning measures (Cello).**

4. The next soprano voice line has three phrases, each set to the text "Osanna in excelsis!" Phrase one starts on beat 2, phrase two on beat 3, and phrase three on a downbeat. Also, the music is *Allegro, forte,* and *marcato*. Determine the best form of preparation for the opening attack and the two subsequent phrase attacks. Identify places that give you trouble and extract them for drill. If you cannot sing the melody, chant it rhythmically and stylistically as you practice conducting the passage.

MUSICAL EXAMPLE 4–4. **Mozart, Requiem, No. 10, Sanctus, final measures (Soprano).**

Right- and Left-Hand Cues for On-Beat Entrances

Your practice with the previous musical examples has enabled you to develop skill in using the appropriate preparatory motion in the right hand to communicate phrase attacks in one voice line or synchronous attacks in all parts. This skill now can be expanded to communicate phrase attacks in any voice line in a musical score and to do so with either the right or left hand. The preparatory gesture signaling an initial attack of a voice serves as an entrance cue and is usually given at the first entrance of that part in the piece and after a period of rest over several beats or measures. Effective cues for an on-beat entrance given in either hand have three characteristics. First, the conducting gesture has the form of a full preparatory beat for the attack. Second, the preparatory motion is directed toward the source of sound—the players or singers who must respond. Third, eye contact with the section or individual making the entrance accompanies, or precedes, the preparatory beat.

Right-hand cues. Entrance cues to voice parts located to the right of the conductor usually are given with the right hand. The right hand also can be used interchangeably with the left to cue parts more or less in front of the conductor. Mechanics of the preparatory motion are exactly the same as those shown in Figures 4–1 and 4–2 for preparing on-beat attacks, with an added feature regarding visibility of the preparation. You must think in terms of moving up or down the base line (Figure 3–4) at which the attack ictus occurs so that the entire movement will be visible to (directed toward) those who must see it, or "read" it. A cue given to those farther away or elevated on risers might require a base line for the ictus (and preparatory beat) that is at chest or chin level, whereas one directed to right-front performers could be at or slightly below normal home base.

Cues given within the context of disciplined conducting should not result in thrusting, pointing, or jabbing gestures; such motions are usually poorly timed and unsightly. Your gestures should be contained within the principles of vertical and lateral planes of movement, relative to your torso, that were introduced in Chapter Two. Rotate your body a few degrees to right or left as necessary to keep your beat pattern essentially in front of you.

Left-hand cues. Giving entrance cues to voice parts in front or to the left of the conductor is one of the important functions of the left hand. (Crossing the body with either hand to give a cue to the opposite side results in an awkward and unacceptable gesture.) Independent uses of the left hand, such as for cueing, involve its activation and deactivation. When the left arm is out of action, it is carried in one of two positions: extended downward alongside the body, or bent at the elbow with the hand held lightly against the body at approximately the lower rib cage.

Activation of the left hand from either position for an entrance cue is a matter of exact timing and form. Correct timing requires that the preparatory motion start from the at-rest home base (carrying position) immediately following the preceding ictus in the right-hand beat, and that it move in the form of a full preparatory beat that arrives at the attack ictus on an imaginary base line well in view of those who make the attack. Figure 4–3 shows two forms of a left-hand cue. One is essentially preparation for a downbeat ictus; the other strokes farther to the outside. Form *a* can be used for an entrance attack on any beat of the measure, but it is particularly easy to coordinate with the continuing right-hand beat pattern for attacks on counts 1 and 3. Form *b* is merely a variation of *a* and might coordinate more easily with the right hand for attacks on beat 2 (to the outside). You must remember that during left-hand cues the right hand continues its beat pattern without interruption. Deactivation of the left hand can occur at any point soon after the rebound from the attack ictus.

Are both hands ever used together to prepare a phrase attack or entrance? Yes, but only sparingly and in well-chosen places. Avoidance of duplication of right-hand movement by the left remains a basic principle of conducting. Both hands (with the left a mirror action of the right) are used simultaneously by many skilled conductors in situations such as these: the preparatory stance and preparatory beat for a beginning *tutti* attack, preparation for an extremely forceful attack or accent, and cueing a large segment of an ensemble (such as all strings in an orchestra, or all male voices in a chorus).

FIGURE 4–3. Left-Hand Attack Cues

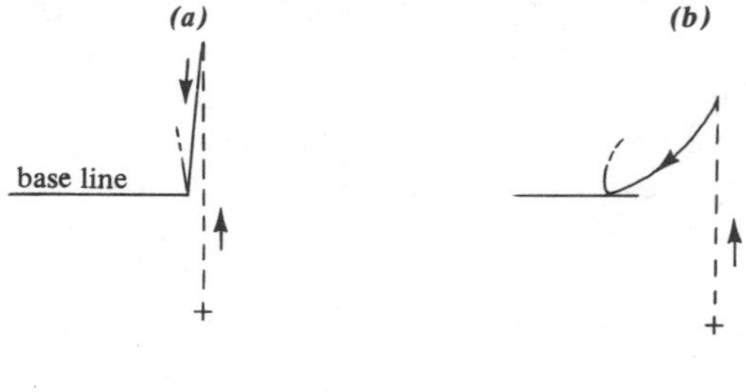

Exercises for practice. Reference already has been made to the point that an entrance cue in either hand should have a full preparatory motion and clear ictus, and it should be directed—along with eye contact—toward the section of the ensemble making the attack. Practicing with an imaginary ensemble divided into areas representing sections can help you acquire the anticipations and coordinations involved, for you must anticipate where the sound is to come from and coordinate all movement with correct timing to signal the response. Figure 4–4 represents a rough geometric area covered by an ensemble (band, orchestra, choir) and is divided into five voice (sectional) areas labeled V1, V2, V3, V4, and V5. Direct your cues and eye contact to the appropriate section while practicing the following exercises and the next musical examples.

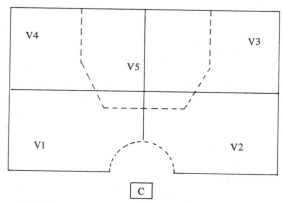

FIGURE 4–4. Imaginary Practice Ensemble

1. Practice the timing and coordination involved in giving left-hand cues by counting one full measure of beats to set a tempo and, in the second measure, activating the left hand to cue an entrance on each beat in turn in a three-beat measure (Figure 4–5). Do not employ the right hand in this exercise.

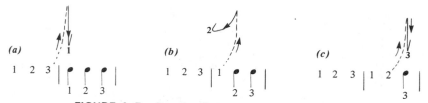

FIGURE 4–5. Practice Patterns for Left-Hand Cues

2. Repeat the previous exercise, but have the right hand maintain the three-beat pattern while the left gives cues as before. Predetermine the section (Figure 4–4) to be cued and direct your attention accordingly.

3. Practice conducting the following nonpitch exercises, which include opening attacks and entrance cues along with tempo and dynamic markings. Direct your right-hand (*RH*) or left-hand (*LH*) cues to the voice locations in Figure 4–4. Attacks marked *RLH* can be prepared with both hands functioning together.

    a. The preparatory stance and opening attack in all parts of this exercise can be managed by the right hand alone, or with right and left hands together as an option. Continuation of voice parts 2 and 3 (located to your right) in measure 3 can be cued by the right hand following form *b*, Figure 4–2. Voices 1 and 4 (to the left) can be cued two measures later by the left hand using form *a*, Figure 4–3.

    b. When the beginning attack is in only one voice line, prepare the attack with your right hand—regardless of whether that voice is located on your right or left. Rotate your body so that you are facing the section making the attack—slightly to your left in this exercise. Keep your attention with voice 1 until you cross the second bar line, at which time your eye contact and right-hand preparation (form *c*, Figure 4–2) should be directed toward voice 2 (right front). Both hands can be used together for cueing voices 3 and 4, which cover an entire left-to-right segment of the ensemble. You should raise the base line for this cue so that it will be visible to the voice parts that are farthest away.

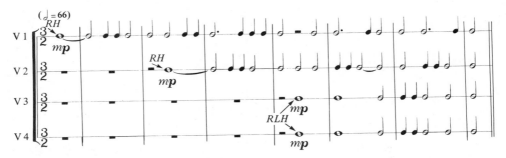

    c. Make all of your own decisions about how to conduct the next exercise and practice conducting it that way.

Musical examples for study and practice. The next quotations from musical scores will give you some initial experiences in executing opening attacks and entrance cues. Play through each excerpt on a piano to familiarize yourself with its sound, and then conduct it, applying techniques and gestures used in the preceding exercises.

1. Musical Example 4–5 is for mixed chorus, and you may assume a seating arrangement in which soprano, alto, tenor, and bass sections have the locations of voice parts 1, 2, 3, and 4, respectively, in Figure 4–4. All of the first three entrances could be prepared with the right hand, and the bass entrance could be handled effectively with a left-hand cue. Remember to shift eye contact to the entering sections and to raise the base line for cues to tenors and basses.

MUSICAL EXAMPLE 4–5. **Bach, Motet VI, Lobet den Herrn, alle Heiden, Alleluja, beginning measures.**

2. Practice the first seven measures of Musical Example 4–6 for the purpose of gaining control of legato and staccato articulations along with the sense of phrasing in the melodic motives and phrases. Next, conduct the entire excerpt, giving

49

cues for each entrance with the right hand: violas and cellos, right front; contra-basses farthest away to the right side. Conduct with each statement of the melody until time to prepare the next entrance.

MUSICAL EXAMPLE 4–6.   **Beethoven, Symphony No. 1 in C Major, Movement II, beginning measures (Strings).**

3. Conduct the next familiar excerpt at a moderate *Allegro* tempo, at a *forte* dynamic level, and in marcato style. Cue the women's voices in measure 3 with a preparation and attack in both hands—left-hand form *b*, Figure 4–3, added to right-hand form *c*, Figure 4–2. Turn your attention to the sopranos in measure 8, and prepare their attack on the downbeat with either hand. Entrances of the other three voice parts on beat 2 in the next measure can be handled like the first entrance of the women's voices.

MUSICAL EXAMPLE 4–7.   **Handel, The Messiah, No. 4, And the Glory of the Lord, measures 51–63 (Chorus).**

INTERNAL ON-BEAT ATTACKS

Thus far we have dealt only with preparations for attacks on the first note of a phrase and applied this preparatory-beat technique to initial phrase attacks, subsequent phrase attacks, and cues given with either hand for entering attacks. In the fullest sense, the start of every tone within a phrase is an attack of that sound, and we shall call them *internal attacks*. Many internal attacks require no special communication by the conductor, for they happen at the right time and in the correct way with relation to the beat pattern and normal ongoing progression of sounds and silences. Some kinds of musical situations within a phrase, however, might need the conductor's attention in order for the ensemble to realize aesthetic qualities intrinsic to the music.

Aesthetic effects in music depend largely on the flux between points of stress and relaxation in a progression of musical sounds. Points of relatively greater stress or accent within a phrase constitute the category to which we will give special consideration at this time. Metrical organization in music is based on the principle that the ongoing tempo beat is organized into accent groupings in which a strong first beat is followed by one or more weaker beats, resulting in duple and triple meters as well as various multiples and combinations of these. Even the conductor's normal beat pattern represents the first beat as stronger because of its direction (straight down) and its greater length. But, as every musician knows, the first beat in a measure is not accented merely because it is the first beat, except in certain dance music and marches. Composers continuously shift stress to other parts of the measure in the ways they organize the flow of sound within a motive, a phrase, or a longer section.

Figure 4–6 presents some typical situations (you should learn to recognize them at sight in a score) that shift the accent or stress from beat 1 to beats 2 or 3 in a three-beat measure. Communication of these effects depends on preparation for a relatively stronger attack on the beat involved and employs the already applied techniques of enlarging the preparatory motion in the right-hand beat pattern and/ or activating the left hand to signal the timing and weight of the attack. Of course, accents falling on the first beat of a measure also need a larger than usual preparatory motion. Study and practice the various illustrations displayed in Figure 4–6 and in Musical Examples 4–8 through 4–12.

Musical Examples for Study and Practice

Marked accents (Figure 4–6). Notes intended for specific accentuation are written with an accent sign or an abbreviation such as *fz* (*forzando* or *forzato*), *sf,* (*sforzando*), and *sfz* (*sforzato*). Accents carry no absolute weight but are relative to their musical context. In lyrical music at a *piano* dynamic, the stress is light but greater than the amount given notes preceding and following the accent. A *sforzato*, on the other hand, is a hard accent that stands out and is normally followed by softer sounds.

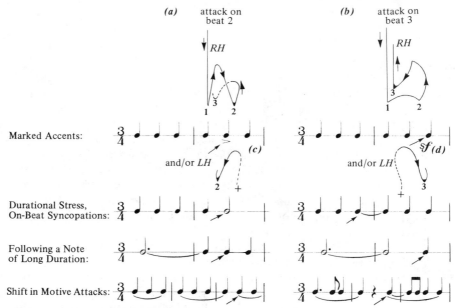

FIGURE 4-6. **Internal On-Beat Attacks**

Musical Example 4–8 has a *sforzando* written on the third beat of several measures. Allow the staccato beat on count 2 in these measures to be relatively light so a larger preparatory motion can be made from that ictus into beat 3.

MUSICAL EXAMPLE 4–8. **Haydn, Symphony No. 104 in D Major, Movement III, beginning measures (Violin 1).**

Half notes in the final measures of Musical Example 4–9 are marked *forzando* and receive their accented attacks on beat 2 preceded by heavy eighth notes on beat 1. Try conducting these measures with a strong staccato beat on 1, a large preparation and heavy attack on 2, and much less motion on 3. Activating the left hand (Figure 4–6c) to function with the right in preparation for the first *forzando* chord might contribute to communication of the hard accent.

MUSICAL EXAMPLE 4–9. **Schubert, Symphony No. 8 in B Minor (Unfinished), Movement I, measures 82–87 (Strings).**

Durational stress (Figure 4–6). Notes of longer duration in the midst of shorter notes usually receive greater stress. In some situations a kind of on-beat syncopation occurs when the longer duration starts on a normally weak beat of the measure (beats 2 or 3 in triple meter). In other cases there is a sense of a change in meter from triple to duple. Beats in the first two complete measures (and other similar places) in Musical Example 4–10 combine into a stress-relaxation pattern of **one**-*two*-**three**-*one*-**two**-*three,* which creates a feeling of duple meter (strong-weak). Try communicating the stressed attacks within your three-beat conducting pattern by minimizing beats two, tied one, and three.

MUSICAL EXAMPLE 4–10. **Mozart, Symphony No. 40 in G Minor, Movement III, beginning measures (Violin 1).**

Following a note of long duration (Figure 4–6). Preparing for an attack of the first note following a note of long duration in the midst of a phrase is primarily a matter of signaling the exact moment at which the sound moves forward so that it will do so with clarity, precision, and appropriate stress. The note may or may not be accented. Singers and players sometimes get careless and lose track of how long they should hold notes of several beats or measures. A preparatory motion following the last ictus of a note's duration provokes a psychological reaction to go ahead on the next beat, even though the count might have been lost. In Musical Example 4–11, move into the tied pitches (measures 3 and 8) with a small, light downbeat, and use a relatively larger preparatory motion into beat 2. Eye contact with the voice section should be an integral part of your reaction as a conductor to these kinds of musical situations.

MUSICAL EXAMPLE 4–11. **Brahms, Requiem, No. IV, How Lovely is Thy Dwelling-Place, measures 25–33 (Tenor).**

Motive attacks (Figure 4–6). Some passages in music are structured around motives of a few notes each. Repetitions or variations of a motive might be accompanied by shifting its start to different positions in the meter (measure). Correct preparation for the beat upon which the motive begins signals its attack and communicates a feeling of the shift in rhythmic stress. Musical Example 4–12 shows an excerpt in which the momentum of motives starting on beat 1 is interrupted by the modulatory chord prior to the double bar and change of key signature. The next three-note motive (new theme) begins without interruption on beat 3 and continues in rhythmic repetitions. You should relax your beat through the tied notes preceding the change of key and prepare (possibly with both hands) for attack of the new thematic motive on beat 3. Relative stress on the third beat, followed by relaxation on the first and second, represents the musical sense of this motive.

MUSICAL EXAMPLE 4–12. **Brahms, Symphony No. 3 in F Major, Movement III, measures 48–55 (Flutes).**

SHAPING PHRASES

Expressiveness or sensitivity in musical performance is the result of responding with feeling, as well as with knowledge and skill, to the fluxes and changes among the musical elements that serve as vehicles for unfolding musical events throughout a composition. Feeling (emotion) in music is a subjective reaction of the human organism to organized sounds and silences. This internal quality is an essential part of aesthetic response. The psychological dimensions of aesthetic experience (based in real-life experience) are in the form of continual adjustments between opposing and dynamic conditions of sound in motion: stress and relaxation, tension and resolution, excitement and calm.

Fulfillment of the aesthetic-dramatic content of a piece of music begins with the conductor's recognizing and reacting to stress-relaxation forces within phrases. Musical phrases are malleable forms that can be fashioned according to the ever-changing flow of sound. For this reason, a pattern of conducting that is merely "time-beating" measure after measure will not suffice to communicate expressive qualities in the music. You already have begun to represent through your conducting movements some of the factors that communicate feeling: levels of loudness, styles of articulation, phrase attacks, and shifts of stress within a phrase line. We now will consider a few additional components of phrase construction that should assist you in shaping phrases as you conduct. These features include contour, variable dynamics, and relative durations.

Phrase Contour

Contour of a phrase is the result of the direction of its pitch movement. The concept of contour can be applied to any horizontal voice line, but it is most often thought of in relation to melodic or thematic phrases. If you were to trace a solid line through the principal note heads of a melody, omitting repetitions and small detours, you probably would produce a graphic representation of contour similar to one shown in Figure 4–7.

A general principle of aesthetic affects of pitch movement is that ascending pitch creates tension and descending pitch brings relaxation. (Obviously, because of all of the variable elements that make up a musical work of art, exceptions to this principle occur.) An ascending pitch line ordinarily requires a degree of increased loudness communicated by a gradual increase in length and weight of the beat; conversely, a descending pitch line often is accompanied by a decrease in loudness, represented through gradually shorter and lighter beats. Angular pitch movement usually creates tension and needs a vigorous beat, whereas pitch lines characterized by numerous repeated pitches, or by only slight fluctuations above and below a principal pitch, produce a feeling of calm, which can be projected with a light beat. Musical Examples 4–13 to 4–17 provide illustrations of some phrase contours.

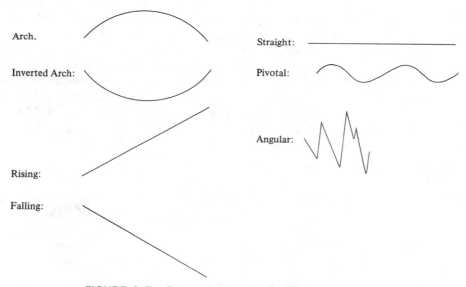

FIGURE 4–7. Representative Phrase Contours

Variable Dynamics

Many musical passages are intended to be performed at a relatively fixed dynamic level (such as *forte, mezzo piano*). The conductor must sustain that level, allowing only for changes necessary to shape the phrases and create intended points of stress such as accents. Other passages in music depend for some of their aesthetic-dramatic content on deliberate changes in loudness. One type of change is abrupt; the other is gradual.

Another function of the left hand used independently from the right is to communicate changes in loudness. Figures 4–8 and 4–9 picture basic left-hand gestures for soft (less sound) and loud (more sound) respectively. *Subito piano* refers to a sudden change from loud to soft, and *subito forte* means suddenly loud. Timing of the gestures is extremely important. To go suddenly from *forte* to *piano* you should activate the left hand immediately following the preceding *forte* ictus, and bring it quickly into a stationary position, with palm toward the players or singers, prior to the *piano* attack. A *subito forte* gesture is timed in the same way, but the left hand arrives in its position either with palm upward or in a clenched fist. These left-hand movements must be synchronized with an appropriate change in the size and weight of the ongoing right-hand beat. Deactivate the left hand as soon as the new dynamic level has been established. Musical Examples 4–15 and 4–16 give you experiences in using left-hand gestures for soft and loud.

Gradual changes in loudness, indicated by markings for *crescendo* and *decrescendo* (or *diminuendo*), can be communicated with the right hand alone by gradually increasing or decreasing the size and weight of the beat. Addition of the left hand also can be very effective for this purpose. You can make a *diminuendo* gesture by activating the left hand and bringing it into a position similar to, but higher than, that shown in Figure 4–8 and continuing with a smooth descending motion through the duration of the decrease in loudness. A *crescendo* gesture begins with bringing the hand smoothly into a position and shape similar to that in Figure 4–9 and continuing to move the hand in an ascending direction until the peak of loudness is reached. Practice conducting Musical Examples 4–13 and 4–16 for experience in using the left hand to assist in communicating a gradual increase or decrease in the dynamic level.

FIGURE 4–8. Left-Hand Gesture for Less Sound

FIGURE 4–9. Left-Hand Gesture for More Sound.

Relative Durations

You will recall that illustrations of durational stress were presented in Figure 4–6 and in some of the musical examples related to that topic. Situations shown were ones in which the position of relatively longer notes in a measure tended to cause a shift of stress or accent away from the first beat and required a preparatory motion to set out their attack. Feeling the appropriate response to notes of longer duration, if and where they occur in a phrase, also is a significant aspect of shaping that phrase. Normally, notes of longer duration at the beginning or in the midst of a phrase (unless marked otherwise) require a stretching or expanding of their sound into the next note. This effect differs from stressing the attack of the note, for an expansion of sound comes as a slight crescendo following the attack and should be communicated by pulling the right hand through a slightly enlarging beat pattern.

Phrase endings create various situations. The primary goal of all pitch movement through a phrase is its cadence, for the ending of a phrase serves as a musical punctuation—light, heavy, short, long—and becomes an important aesthetic ingredient. Cadences frequently are points of resolution and relaxation, but at other times they are stressful and dramatic. The size, weight, and style of your beat should reflect the nature of the cadence, whatever that might be. In one case a cadence of long duration might be so calm as to need very little motion in the conducting beat; in another circumstance a sustained ending could be the climax of a phrase and demand forceful conducting through its entire duration. Similarly, cadences on notes of short duration can be either very light and relaxed or heavy and percussive. You should be attentive in responding to relative durations at the beginning, within, and at the end of phrases as you practice conducting the next musical examples.

Musical Examples for Study and Practice in Shaping Phrases

1. Musical Example 4–13 contains two four-measure phrases with an arch contour in each. Conduct the excerpt with only the right hand and attempt to communicate a *crescendo-decrescendo* that follows the phrase contours by increasing and decreasing the size of your beat pattern. Both the *crescendo* in phrase one and the *sforzando* in phrase two are relative to a *piano* dynamic level. Remember also to relax your beat on the cadence in measure 4 and give a good preparatory motion for the phrase attack on beat 1 in measure 5.

MUSICAL EXAMPLE 4–13. Mendelssohn, Symphony No. 3 in A Minor (Scotch), Movement I, beginning measures (Violas).

2. Study the next soprano melody (Musical Example 4–14). *Crescendo* and *decrescendo* markings have been omitted and you may depend entirely on following

phrase contour to conduct expressively. Some conductors would prefer to think of this excerpt as one long phrase; others might decide on light phrasings with punctuations in the text. In either case the melody has an arch shape that arrives at the highest pitch, longest duration, and most important word in measure 5. Start with a small legato beat pattern, increase its size between measures 2 and 5, maintain the peak through the dotted-half note, and start a decrease when the pitch begins to descend. A slight expansion of sound on the repetition of *Lord* (measure 8) would be appropriate to a concept of shaping the entire passage.

MUSICAL EXAMPLE 4–14.   Brahms, Requiem, No. IV, How Lovely Is Thy Dwelling-Place, beginning measures (Soprano).

3. Prepare for a *forte* attack on beat 3 and continue at that level through the downbeat in measure 4 of Musical Example 4–15. Use a small stroke into a light ictus on the quarter rest and immediately activate your left hand into a *subito piano* position while your right prepares the phrase attack on beat 3. Practice only measures 3–5 until all movement is well coordinated.

MUSICAL EXAMPLE 4–15.   Haydn, Symphony No. 101 in D Major (Clock), Movement III, beginning measures (Violin 1).

4. Communicate the *crescendo* from *piano* to *forte* (Musical Example 4–16) through a gradual increase of length and weight in your right-hand beat. Activate the left hand in a gesture for sustaining more sound (Figure 4–9) on the downbeat of measure 5. Keep a firm right-hand beat into the ictus of beat 1, measure 6, and immediately reduce the rebound while rolling the left hand over into a *piano* gesture. Continue a light right-hand beat on counts 2 and 3.

MUSICAL EXAMPLE 4–16.   Beethoven, Symphony No. I in C Major, Movement II, measures 89–97 (Violin 1).

5. The opening theme in Musical Example 4–17 ends in a very soft note of three measures' duration. This type of phrase ending can be conducted by merely keeping a very light beat pulsation stretching in a sustaining manner toward the outside instead of using a succession of beat patterns with a more pronounced downbeat. You should move in a larger preparatory motion from the last ictus of the sustained note to cue the violins' entrances.

MUSICAL EXAMPLE 4–17. **Schubert, Symphony No. 8 in B Minor (Unfinished), Movement I, beginning measures.**

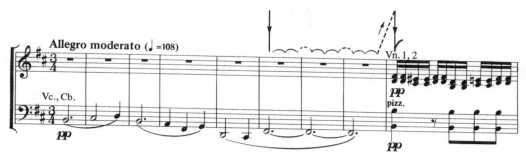

Releases and Fermatas

RELEASES

The term *release* refers to the stopping or cutting off of sound, and the conducting gesture that signals cessation of sound is called a *release*, or *cut-off*. A conductor's ability to control important releases in the voice lines is as important to overall skills as the proper handling of attacks. The presentation of release techniques will discuss the form of the motion, applications in the three-beat pattern, timing of the release, and musical applications and examples for practicing releases.

Form

Release gestures are usually described as looping motions. Although the loop is a continuous movement, it can be separated into the component parts shown in Figure 5–1. A release motion might start from either a hold position on a fermata or the ictus point of a preceding beat in an ongoing beat pattern. The complete gesture begins as if it were a rebound from the starting point, strokes to a downward-most point that looks like an ictus, and concludes with a follow-through that looks like a rebound or recoil. Correct timing of the release of sound is provided by the preparatory motion leading to an ictus point, and the actual cessation of sound probably coincides with the follow-through.

Release loops can take on various forms, including elliptical, circular, and downbeat shapes. Furthermore, elliptical and circular motions can move in either an inside or outside direction, and all forms can be applied in either hand. Some of the varieties of form and direction are shown in Figure 5–2.

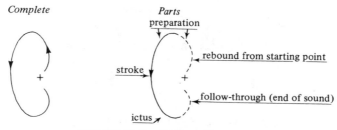

Complete   Parts

preparation

rebound from starting point

stroke

follow-through (end of sound)

ictus

FIGURE 5-1. Release Gesture

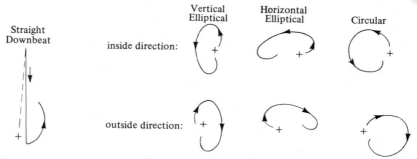

Straight
Downbeat

Vertical
Elliptical

Horizontal
Elliptical

Circular

inside direction:

outside direction:

FIGURE 5-2. Forms of Right-Hand Release Gestures

Applications to the Three-Beat Pattern

Most releases must be made within the context of the conductor's beat pattern. A three-beat pattern might have releases on the downbeat, on beat 2 to the outside, or on the final beat. The release technique substitutes a release gesture—modified to suit the conducting motion at that point—for a normal beat of the continuing pattern. One fundamental rule is to use a form and direction that will leave you in the best position to continue into the next ictus of the regular beat pattern, unless the release is one which ends the piece or movement. Figure 5-3 shows acceptable releases on each beat of a three-beat pattern.

Figure 5-4 shows a basic left-hand release gesture. Whereas the right hand alone can communicate many cut-offs, the left hand becomes a highly effective

FIGURE 5-3. Releases in a Three-Beat Pattern

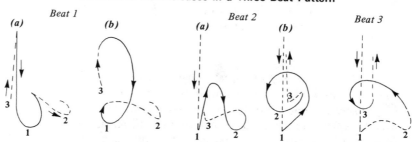

Beat 1

Beat 2

Beat 3

(a)   (b)   (a)   (b)

FIGURE 5-4. Left-Hand Release Gesture

vehicle for release of sound in two kinds of cases. Conductors sometimes use both hands for such purposes as release of a fermata, release before a major interruption or break, and final releases. In these cases left-hand gestures duplicate and mirror those of the right hand. Any of the forms shown in Figures 5-2 and 5-3 can be used with hands working together. The left hand also can be employed separately from the right and give the primary gesture. Independent left-hand releases are especially useful as phrasing gestures and to release one or more voice lines while others continue.

    Practice excercises. You should practice introducing a release loop into your basic three-beat conducting pattern before continuing. Fundamental technique in right-hand releases involves rebounding from the preceding ictus in a way that will bring the release loop into full view of the ensemble and will allow the follow-through to continue into the next beat of the pattern. Your entire motion, along with the associated eye contact, can be directed toward the whole ensemble or any part of it. When using your left hand for the primary release gesture, activate it in the same timing as a preparatory motion for attack and continue its movement in a release loop similar to that shown in Figure 5-4. Deactivate the left hand at the end of its follow-through. You can begin to acquire coordination and form of movement by doing the following exercises (practice before a mirror and chant the beat as written while you conduct):

1. Right hand alone (Figure 5-3):
   a. on beat 1, form *a*: one-two-three, *release*-two-three
   b. on beat 1, form *b*: one-two-three, *release*-two-three
   c. on beat 2, form *a*: one-two-three, one-*release*-three
   d. on beat 2, form *b*: one-two-three, one-*release*-three
   e. on beat 3:   one-two-three, one-two-*release*, one.
2. Activation of left hand for primary release gesture (Figure 5-4); right hand keeps regular beat pattern:
   a. on beat 1: one-two-three, *release*-two-three
   b. on beat 2: one-two-three, one-*release*-three
   c. on beat 3: one-two-three, one-two-*release*, one.

Timing

    A precise release of sound depends largely on two factors: its exact point in time and the corresponding duration of the release motion.

    Point in time. During your study of the score you should have determined exactly when sound should cease at important release points throughout the piece. Competent composers and arrangers carefully select note values to represent the exact durations they conceived. Your responsibility is to reproduce what was written, for to do otherwise might change the intended musical effect.

Both the note to be released and its corresponding release gesture can occupy either a full count's duration or only the first part of a count. Figure 5–5 represents the most usual points in time for releases in triple meter. Releases of sounds whose final duration occupies only the first part of a count usually present no particular barrier to performing and conducting them as written. Sound written to continue through a full count sometimes requires a choice from among two or three options for the most appropriate point of release. One such situation is illustrated in Figure 5–6.

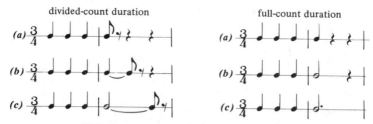

FIGURE 5–5. Notated Release Points

FIGURE 5–6. Performance Options for Point of Release

Which performance option in Figure 5–6 is correct? It depends on the musical situation. If the sound ends a phrase that is followed by a new phrase attack on the next beat, a phrasing release such as option *c* would be appropriate. Option *b*, which actually carries the sound into the next beat, would be a bad choice if it were to extend the pitch from one or more voice parts into an unwritten dissonance with other pitches—in the accompaniment or other voices—on the next beat. On the other hand, *b* might work well as a final release to some sections or pieces of music. The best rule in most musical situations, however, is to release the sound exactly as notated, which in this case is at the end of count 3, at the bar line as shown in option *a*, and immediately prior to the point of the next ictus.

Duration of release motion. Release gestures are applied by inserting them into the ongoing beat pattern, as shown in Figure 5–3. Ideally, sound should end at the same moment the release gesture is completed. You must realize that the ictus point of the release loop (Figure 5–1) corresponds in time to the beat ictus that starts the count during which the sound is released. That part of the motion preceding the ictus is preparatory. Duration of the follow-through relates to duration of sound in the final beat or count. Therefore, proper timing includes regulating the speed and length of the follow-through to match the duration of sound being released. In Figure 5–7, examples *a* and *c* are quicker and shorter than examples *b* and *d*. You also should keep in mind that release gestures, as well as preparations for attacks, must always be made in keeping with the tempo, dynamic level, and style of the music; hence, exact size and speed of the follow-through are relative. Practice each of the examples in Figure 5–7.

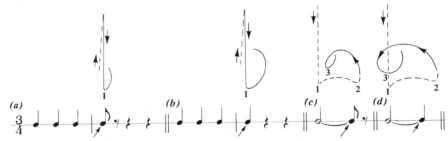

FIGURE 5–7. Follow-Through Durations

Musical Applications

When preparing a score for conducting, you should identify places where release motions might be needed to assure proper timing and precision of releases of sound during performance. You also should determine whether the right or left hand, or both hands, will be used to give the primary release gesture, as well as which voice part or parts are involved in the release. The five musical situations most likely to require a conductor's attention are: final releases, releases of a fermata, releases preceding rests, releases preceding a break, and phrasing releases.

Final releases. Final releases are those that end a piece, a movement, or a major section closed with a double bar line. A release gesture is always required at these points, and techniques for handling the cut-off are based on several factors.

Both hands in equal movement are used by conductors on many final releases. You may employ either the inside or outside direction for a final release, but a large outside motion is particularly impressive on forceful endings. Heavy (loud, marked) releases often call for a straight or elliptical downbeat form, regardless of the count of the measure on which they occur. Circular or elliptical forms are appropriate for light (soft, legato) endings.

Final releases (except in the case of fermatas) are given on the final beat of the final note's duration. In case of a final *ritardando* or *accelerando*, duration of the release motion and follow-through should be in the retarded or accelerated tempo. After a final release concluding a piece, allow a slight pause to occur before dropping both hands to the sides.

Musical examples for study and practice. The next three musical excerpts demonstrate conditions surrounding final releases. Refer to Figures 5–2 and 5–7 for help in selecting and applying a workable form for each case.

1. Musical Example 5–1 moves to the final chord at an *Allegro* tempo, *forte* dynamic, and in marcato style. A straight downbeat form (Figure 5–2) delivered in marcato style will function well, but you also might want to try a vertical elliptical form in both an inside and outside direction. Add the left hand to the right, in the same form of release, by activating it at the rebound from the ictus of beat 3 preceding the final chord.

MUSICAL EXAMPLE 5–1. **Mozart, Symphony No. 39 in E Flat Major, Movement I, final measures (Strings).**

2. The final chord in Musical Example 5–2 fills one beat's duration and presents the same options for a final release as Example 5–1. However, changes in dynamics and punctuations caused by one-beat silences bring additional challenges.

MUSICAL EXAMPLE 5–2. **Beethoven, Symphony No. 5 in C Minor, Movement II, final measures (Woodwinds).**

Beat 1 preceding the first eighth rest in Example 5–2 can be treated as a downbeat release motion (Figure 5–3). Continue with a very small stroke and light ictus on the rest (count 2); then enlarge your preparatory motion leading to a staccato and *piano* attack of the chords on beats 3 and 1. Following the second eighth rest, prepare for a *forte* attack on beat 3, and continue with a forceful beat into the final release.

3. Musical Example 5–3 ends the exposition section of a sonata-allegro movement and closes with double bars and a repeat sign. The last note on beat 2 can be treated as a final release of this section. Try all three forms of release illustrated with the excerpt until you have control of each; then choose the one you prefer. Repetition of the exposition starts on the next measure, so you must be in a position at the end of your follow-through to observe the rest on beat 3 and move in tempo with a preparatory motion for an attack on the next downbeat.

MUSICAL EXAMPLE 5-3.   Mozart, Symphony No. 39 in E Flat Major, Movement I, measures 140-143 (Violin 1 and 2).

Releases preceding rests. Silences are an integral part of musical aesthetics; handling them effectively requires skill on the part of any performer, including conductors. The primary principle for conducting rests of one or two beats in duration (rests of longer duration are presented in Chapter Twelve) is to refrain from continuing beats of the same weight, length, and form through the silence, for to do so creates an aural-visual conflict: No sound occurs, but the conductor keeps beating time as though it were supposed to continue.

Rests for one or two beats can be conducted by applying one of two techniques. A minibeat (small stroke) might be used to mark the ictus of each beat of silence if maintaining a feeling of tempo and pulse through the rest is considered necessary (as in a very slow tempo). A "negated beat" also functions very well in some cases of only one or two beats of silence. Negation of a beat requires omitting its ictus completely, and the technique involves coming to an arrest (stop) at the top of the rebound of the beat preceding the rest, holding the arrest position through each beat omitted, and moving with a preparatory motion for the next attack of sound immediately after you feel the ictus that would have occurred on the beat of silence. Figure 5-8 illustrates the minibeat and the negated beat.

FIGURE 5-8.   **Conducting Release-Rest-Attack**

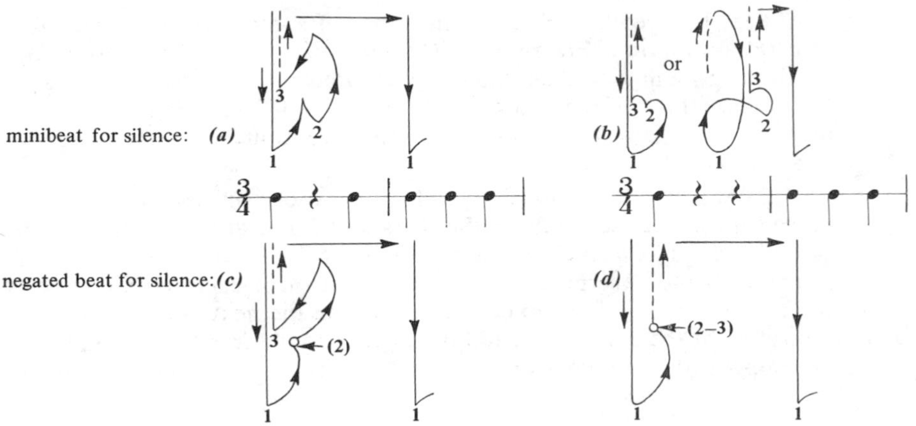

minibeat for silence: *(a)*

(b)

negated beat for silence: *(c)*

(d)

The beat motion preceding a rest often functions as a release of that sound and clears the air for silence. This is especially true when the rest separates two units such as phrases or motives, and when precision of release, rest, and attack are crucial to the intended musical effect. Figure 5–8 illustrates two applications of minibeats and negated beats for silence, along with preceding releases and following attacks. Practice each situation to achieve coordination and timing. Your left hand can be added at your discretion for any attack or release gesture.

Musical examples for study and practice. Musical Examples 5–4 to 5–6 give you a variety of opportunities to conduct rests, releases preceding rests, and attacks following rests. Try to adapt the forms of releases, minibeats, and negated beats illustrated in Figures 5–2, 5–3, and 5–8 to your study and practice of the excerpts.

1. Consider measures 2 and 3 in Musical Example 5–4 as one problem and measures 4 and 5 another. Beat 2 in measure 2 can be given a heavy and quick release loop patterned after either form *a* or *b* in Figure 5–3. Negate beat 3 and repeat the same actions in measure 3. In measure 4 use a strong downbeat release on beat 1, negate beat 2, move in a small preparatory motion for the *piano* attack on beat 3, and conclude with a final release in the form of a light (staccato) downbeat.

MUSICAL EXAMPLE 5–4. **Beethoven, Symphony No. 2 in D Major, Movement II, final measures (Strings).**

2. Variable dynamics, a very slow tempo, releases, rests, and attacks are all within control of the conductor in Musical Example 5–5. Try to attend the events in the following sequence and ways:

   a. Prepare the *forte* attack on beat 3, measure 1, and cross the bar line with a heavy downbeat (*sforzando*).
   b. Use a left-hand release gesture (Figure 5–4) for the phrase release on beat 2, and try to represent the exact value of the eighth note in the length of your follow-through.
   c. Employ a minibeat on the quarter rest (beat 3, measure 2), and enlarge your preparatory motion into the *piano* attack. This downbeat can be a release loop with a long, slow follow-through occupying the full beat.
   d. Negate beat 2, measure 3, and prepare the attack on beat 3.
   e. A light staccato downbeat in measure 4 will coordinate with the eighth-note value and can be followed by minibeats marking the ictus of beats 2 and 3. Apply a large rebound from the ictus of beat 3 to cross the last bar line with a full preparation for an on-beat *fortissimo* attack.

MUSICAL EXAMPLE 5–5.   **Haydn, Symphony No. 88 in D Major, Movement II, measures 43–47 (Violin 1 and 2).**

3. Conducting Musical Example 5–6 will be easier if you first decide how to release prior to the rests and how to observe the silence. One good possibility is to use a downbeat release loop as shown in Figure 5–7b on the word *nichts* (measures 2 and 3). This gesture should fill the beat's entire duration. Minibeats on the rests are advisable because the total silence is two or three beats at a moderately slow tempo. Following the very light silent downbeat in measure 4, rebound and move with a large preparatory motion for the *forte* attack on beat 2. You could activate your left hand to signal the *mezzo piano* attack in measure 3, and add it to your right in preparing the *forte* attack in measure 4.

MUSICAL EXAMPLE 5–6.   **Bach, Jesu, Meine Freude, No. 2, beginning measures.**

Release preceding a break. From time to time you will encounter places in music where an intentional interruption in the tempo beat is indicated. The beat actually stops for a moment and resumes after a slight pause. One of the two most common indicators of breaks is a fermata sign placed over a bar line or over a rest; the other is a caesura (kay-soo′-rah) sign, which consists of double slash marks across the top line of the staff. You can apply correct technique for conducting either kind of break through a sequence of movements in which you substitute a release gesture for the last beat before the break, finish the follow-through at an arrest position from which the attack after the break can be made easily, pause briefly in the arrest position for observance of the break, and start again with a full preparation for the next attack.

Figure 5–9 and Musical Example 5–7 present some situations that you should practice. The left hand can be activated to augment the right or to give the primary gesture for release. Remember that conducting movements for control of special events such as breaks need to be raised to a level high enough for clear visibility from the ensemble.

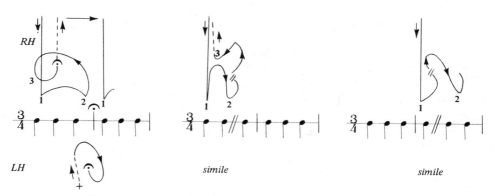

FIGURE 5-9. Conducting Breaks

MUSICAL EXAMPLE 5-7. **Brahms, Symphony No. 2 in D Major, Movement III, measures 21-24 (Woodwinds).**

Phrasing releases. Phrase cadences are points of arrival for the movement of sound through the phrase and serve as musical punctuations that are essential to overall psychological-aesthetic meanings of music. Proper observance of phrase punctuation requires that the performer release the final sound of one phrase and make a clear attack on the next. Phrase releases followed by a break or rest have already been covered, but cadences followed immediately by attack of the next phrase need further consideration.

You need not communicate all phrasings, but you will often find that, while shaping phrases and controlling ensemble precision, you will automatically incorporate forms and gestures in your conducting patterns to show phrase punctuations. Sometimes the phrasing release and attack can be inserted into the right hand's continuing beat pattern in ways similar to movements illustrated in Figure 5-3. At other times a special release gesture in the left hand might help communicate a sense of phrasing to the singers or players. A left-hand phrasing release takes the approximate form of a comma or breath mark traced in the air (Figure 5-4), and it can be given to one or more voice parts in accordance with the musical situation. Time for a phrase punctuation and breath must be taken from the last part of the final beat of a phrase so that attack of the next phrase can occur at its exact moment. You must decide which phrasings are necessary, because attempting release gestures at every cadence would clutter conducting movements.

Figure 5–10 shows phrasing release-attack gestures for each point in a three-beat measure. Study options of using the right hand alone or activating the left hand to give the primary phrase release while the right continues its beat pattern. Practice each situation illustrated.

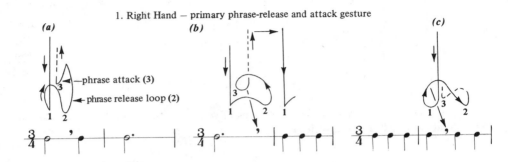

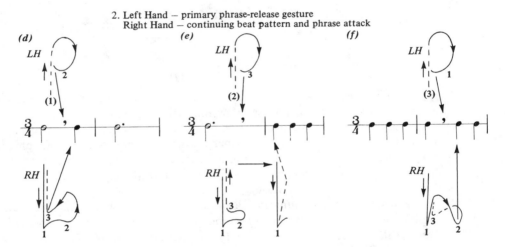

FIGURE 5–10.   Phrasing Release-Attack

Musical examples for study and practice. Musical Examples 5–8 to 5–11 will give you some opportunities to practice right- and left-hand phrasing gestures in musical contexts.

1. The composer has written an eighth rest to accomodate a phrase punctuation and breath at the end of measure 2 in Musical Example 5–8. Your right hand can communicate both a strong release of phrase one and a *fortissimo* attack of phrase two if you adapt the form of beat illustrated in Figure 5–10*b*.

MUSICAL EXAMPLE 5–8. **Gounod, Messe Solennelle, No. V, Sanctus, measures 81–84 (Chorus).**

2. Musical Example 5–9 has a primary melody constructed in four-measure phrases. Practice communicating a phrasing release-attack in measure 4 in two ways: First, use your right hand alone (Figure 5–10*a*); next, activate your left hand to give the phrasing gesture (Figure 5–10*d*).

MUSICAL EXAMPLE 5–9. **Gustav Holst, Jupiter, *from* The Planets, arranged for Military Band, measures 108–115 (condensed score).** ©Copyright 1924 by Boosey & Co.; Renewed 1951. Reprinted by permission of Boosey & Hawkes, Inc.

3. Left-hand phrasing gestures are especially useful to choral directors who strive for precision in the release of final consonants at cadence points. Phrasing at the double bar in Musical Example 5–10 is an excellent situation for you to practice. The relatively slow tempo and further *ritardando* can be controlled through the right-hand beat. Particular attention should be given the lower voice lines, which have the main pitch-rhythm movement. Activate your left hand to give a gentle release gesture, in the slow and retarded tempo, with beat 3 prior to the double bar. Some choral conductors would end this release motion with a "finger release" of the final consonant ("s" given the sound of "z"). A release gesture made with fingers consists of closing the tip of the index finger, and/or middle finger, against the tip of the thumb. Finger releases should be used sparingly, but they are effective in signaling precise timing for articulation of a final consonant. Continue from the phrase release with a right-hand or a two-hand attack of the next phrase at a *piano* level and slightly faster tempo.

MUSICAL EXAMPLE 5–10.   **Heitor Villa-Lobos, Missa Saõ Sebastião (Mass in honor of Saint Sebastian) for three-part chorus, Gloria.** Copyright © 1937 by Associated Music Publishers, Inc. Used by permission.

4. Using your left hand to assist in shaping the phrase ending and release will seem natural in each of the first two phrases of Musical Example 5–11. Each phrase builds through a very slow tempo (legato style) to a stress on the note tied across the bar line and diminishes to the phrase release on an eighth note. Build to the point of stress with your right hand, then activate the left after the ictus of beat 1, measure 2, in a *decrescendo* gesture that descends and ends like a release in the first part of beat 2.

MUSICAL EXAMPLE 5–11.   **Haydn, Symphony No. 88 in G Major, Movement II, beginning measures (Oboe).**

FERMATAS

A fermata—defined as a pause or hold—is a cessation of rhythm during which a discontinuation of the beat occurs. Fermatas are found in two general musical contexts and are interpreted differently in each. First, in early chorales (including those of J. S. Bach), a fermata sign indicates the ending of a phrase rather than an elongation of sound beyond its written duration. Which, if any, of the fermatas in a chorale are to be held is an individual decision of the conductor. Second, fermatas in music other than chorales are used to lengthen a written note for an indeterminate amount beyond its notated duration. The conductor must decide exactly how long to hold each fermata on the basis of his or her feeling for the best aesthetic effect.

Fermatas are special situations in a music score, and their execution requires specific conducting skills. Techniques for controlling a fermata are based on how the hold is entered and how it is left.

Entering a Fermata

The form of the conducting motion for signaling the entrance (attack) of a fermata is composed of three parts, as shown in Figure 5–11. Size of the motion must be somewhat larger, in comparison with those preceding it, to provide a clear visual communication to singers or players of the approach to the hold.

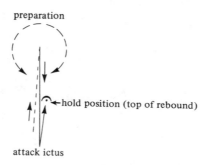

preparation

hold position (top of rebound)

attack ictus

FIGURE 5–11.   Form of a Fermata Attack

You should enter every fermata with (fundamentally) a downbeat, regardless of the beat or count in the measure on which it occurs. The complete entrance gesture of the right hand is similar to a full preparation (starting from the preceding ictus) for a downbeat attack. In some cases the stroke downward also will move slightly to the outside or inside. Stop your hand at the top of the rebound in a hold position from which you will be able either to leave the fermata or, if necessary, continue movement in the form of a *crescendo* or *diminuendo* gesture on the held note.

Entrance to, or attack of, a fermata is on the first beat of the note under the fermata sign. No further beating should occur, regardless of the value of the note, throughout the full duration of the hold. A fermata can start on any count of a measure and on any beat of a conducting pattern. Two general situations are possible in which voice lines have either notes of the same value or notes of different values within the overall duration of a fermata's effect. Figure 5–12 presents points of entrance to fermatas within a three-beat pattern when all voice lines have notes of the same value; Figure 5–13 illustrates attacks when notes of different values occur among the parts.

Conductors often use both hands in controlling an ensemble's performance of a fermata because of the increased visibility (and attention drawn to this special event) that is provided by addition of the left hand. When you elect to use both hands, activate the left during the preparatory motion entering the fermata and allow it to continue functioning with the right through the hold position and movement involved in leaving the fermata. Practice the situations for entering and holding fermatas shown in Figure 5–12 with right hand alone and with hands together.

Both hands generally become involved when two notes of different values appear in different voice lines and each is marked with a fermata sign. Ordinarily you can attack and sustain the note of longer value with the left hand (palm inclined upward) while the right continues to beat into the next note and comes to a hold on it (Figure 5–13a and b). This situation can be altered if, for instance, the

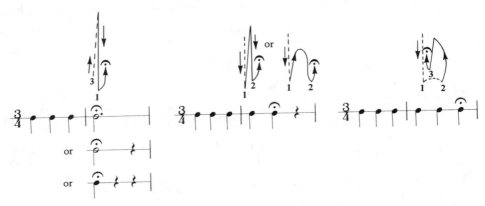

FIGURE 5–12. Fermata Attacks in a Three-Beat Pattern (notes of same value in all parts)

FIGURE 5–13. Fermatas on Notes of Different Values

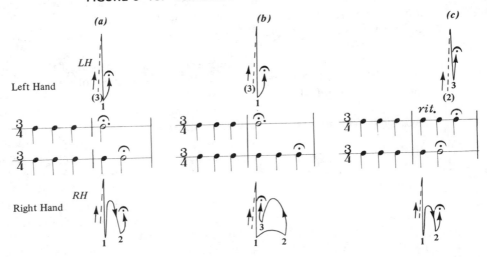

voice that keeps moving is located on the conductor's left and communicating to that section can be done more easily with the left hand (Figure 5–13c).

Leaving Continuation Fermatas

Fermatas can be categorized as those that conclude a piece, movement, or major section and those that occur at other points within the piece. We will first give attention to holds in the midst of a piece, referring to them as *continuation fermatas*. Conditions for leaving a continuation fermata are classified on the basis of whether the hold is followed by a major interruption, a minor interruption, or no interruption. Conducting technique is determined by musical conditions in each classification.

With a major interruption. A major interruption of sound following a fermata within a piece of music is created by events such as a rest of one or more counts duration or by a break (caesura). The technique for conducting these kinds of musical situations requires two separate movements: a complete release terminating the hold and, following a pause, a full preparation for the next attack. You should study and practice each of the illustrations in Figure 5–14.

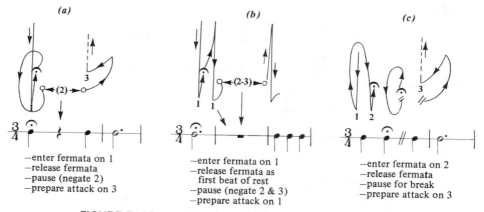

(a)

—enter fermata on 1
—release fermata
—pause (negate 2)
—prepare attack on 3

(b)

—enter fermata on 1
—release fermata as
  first beat of rest
—pause (negate 2 & 3)
—prepare attack on 1

(c)

—enter fermata on 2
—release fermata
—pause for break
—prepare attack on 3

FIGURE 5–14. **Leaving a Fermata with a Major Interruption**

Musical examples for study and practice. Try applying techniques illustrated in Figure 5–14 to conducting the fermatas in Musical Examples 5–12 and 5–13.

1. Pattern your conducting of the fermata and major interruption in Musical Example 5–12 after the illustration in Figure 5–14b. The music is *fortissimo* and marcato; hence, your attack entering the fermata, your release of the hold, and your preparation for the next attack should be large, heavy, and precise. Direct your opening attack to the basses and prepare the attack in measure 4 as an entrance cue to altos and tenors.

MUSICAL EXAMPLE 5–12. **Randall Thompson, The Peaceable Kingdom, No. VII, Have Ye Not Known?, beginning measures.** ©Copyright 1936, by E. C. Schirmer Music Co., Boston. Used by permission.

2. Notes of different values appear with fermata signs in measure 2 of Musical Example 5–13. Enter the fermatas using an adaptation of the form illustrated in Figure 5–13a. Release the holds with both hands, pause for the caesura, and give a right-hand preparation for the next phrase attack on beat 3 (Figure 5–14c).

MUSICAL EXAMPLE 5–13. **Mendelssohn, A Midsummer Night's Dream, Nocturne, measures 25–28.**

With a minor interruption. Fermatas on the last note of a phrase followed by a new phrase attack on the next beat create a minor interruption resulting from the time necessary to observe a phrase punctuation and breath. Conducting technique at these points requires a release of the fermata with a curved or looping gesture and a continuation without arrest into a preparatory motion for the following attack (in tempo). In a sense the fermata release and preparation for attack are one continuous movement. Study carefully the three illustrations in Figure 5–15, which show each release as a somewhat downward loop continuing smoothly into a full preparation for attack on each beat of a three-beat measure. Practice each of these examples.

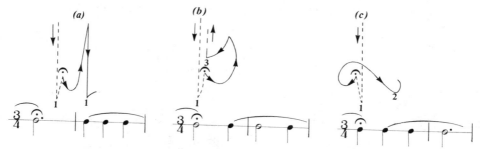

FIGURE 5-15. Leaving Fermatas with a Phrasing Interruption

Musical examples for study and practice. Musical Examples 5–14 to 5–17 provide opportunities for you to practice leaving a fermata with a minor interruption created by a phrasing release and attack.

1. Begin your practice of Musical Example 5–14 with concentration on a very slow legato beat building gradually to a *forte* on the downbeat of measure 3. Reduce the right-hand beat in size through measure 3 and at the same time add a left-hand gesture for *descrescendo*. Allow both hands to enter the fermata, and sustain the hold position beyond a duration of three slow counts. Release the fermata with your right hand (or both hands), and continue motion into the next phrase attack on a downbeat (Figure 5–15*a*).

MUSICAL EXAMPLE 5-14. **Haydn, Symphony No. 101 in D Major, Movement I, beginning measures.**

2. Musical Example 5–15 has fermatas tied over two measures to accommodate the very fast tempo and *crescendo* through the hold. Graphic illustrations have been added to show a way to attack each fermata and continue to increase loudness. The tied eighth note and eighth rest indicate a rhythmic release and phrasing on count 3 and continuation with preparation for an *a tempo* attack on beat 1. You might want to experiment with adding your left hand in a *crescendo* gesture through the hold and leaving it activated through the phrasing release-attack.

MUSICAL EXAMPLE 5–15.   **Jean Berger, Vision of Peace, No. II (Soprano).** Copyright 1949, by Broude Brothers. Used by permission.

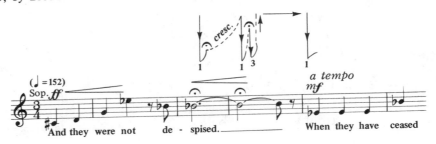

3. *Lunga* (long) written over the fermata sign in Musical Example 5–16 means a hold that is longer than otherwise. Conduct this excerpt using Figure 5–15*b* as a model for your continuation release and attack in leaving the fermata.

MUSICAL EXAMPLE 5–16.   **Brahms, Symphony No. 3 in F Major, Movement III, measures 97–100.**

4. Musical Example 5–17 contains both a continuation fermata with phrasing interruption and one followed by a major interruption in the form of a caesura sign with the word *lunga* over it. Try to determine for yourself exactly how best to conduct this passage, and practice until you feel in complete control. How can you communicate the *mezzo piano* attack following the *fortissimo* hold and caesura?

MUSICAL EXAMPLE 5–17.   **William Bergsma, Riddle Me This, No. 1, Answer: The Snow, beginning measures (Soprano).** © 1957, by Galaxy Music Corporation. Used by permission.

Without interruption. Sometimes a fermata occurs within a phrase and has no separation or detachment between its termination and the next note. Release or cut-off gestures are unnecessary. All that is required is movement from the hold position in a preparatory motion for attack of the next note. Try to avoid starting the preparation in a downward direction, for this motion might be interpreted by players or singers as a release loop and phrasing interruption. Notes under the fermata signs continue to sound through the preparatory gesture and move to the next notes at the attack ictus. Figure 5–16 illustrates situations you can use to practice techniques in leaving fermatas without interruption.

FIGURE 5–16. **Leaving Fermatas Without Interruption**

Musical examples for study and practice. Study the excerpts quoted in Musical Examples 5–18 and 5–19 to gain a full understanding of how the fermatas must be performed, then practice conducting each example with the techniques suggested for it.

1. Musical Example 5–18 has strings entering on a fermata at the same time woodwinds release. Cue the entrance and hold beat 3 with your right hand in the way shown in Figure 5–16c. You might be able to depend on the woodwinds to release with the ictus of the fermata attack; it not, give them a left-hand phrasing release simultaneously with the right-hand attack. This fermata is left without interruption, so continue by moving from the hold position in a full preparation for the next downbeat.

MUSICAL EXAMPLE 5–18. **Brahms, Symphony No. 2 in D Major, Movement III, measures 233–238.**

2. Still another context for fermatas occurs in Musical Example 5–19. Notes of different values appear under fermata signs, but the lowest voice holds on the first note, then moves in rhythm before all voices phrase together.

MUSICAL EXAMPLE 5–19.   **Heitor Villa-Lobos, Missa São Sebastião (Mass in honor of Saint Sebastian) for three-part chorus, Credo.** Copyright © 1937 by Associated Music Publishers, Inc. Used by permission.

You should enter the fermatas in Musical Example 5–19 with both hands, sustain the upper parts with your left (palm up), hold the quarter note with your right hand, then resume (without interruption) your beat pattern on beat 2 (Figure 5–16*a*). Bring both hands into a phrasing release loop with beat 3; thus all parts will phrase together. Continue from the phrasing release with your right hand to cross the double bar for a downbeat attack in the middle voice.

Concluding Fermatas

Many pieces and movements conclude with a fermata. These final holds should be terminated with a cut-off of a size and strength relative to the sound being released. Other decisions about the form of your hold and release gestures must be made on the basis of whether a fixed or variable dynamic level applies through the fermata's entire duration.

Fixed dynamic. Starting to move from a hold position creates a psychological expectation and anticipation of release; it signals the beginning of the preparatory motion for a cut-off. Most releases from a fixed dynamic level, and a hold of relatively short duration, can be made by retaining a stable hold position and timing the full release gesture to correspond to the value of one beat in the tempo that led to the fermata. Ensembles sometimes have a tendency to allow a decrease of sound to happen in holds of longer duration at a loud level. A left-hand sustaining gesture for more sound (Figure 4–9) can be intensified by vibrating the forearm and hand. Addition of this gesture is useful in preventing a loss of intensity of sound during the fermata.

Your release loop from a fixed dynamic level can take any of the forms shown in Figure 5–2. Your choice will depend largely on the style, general mood, and level of loudness of the musical ending. Downbeat or vertical elliptical (inside or outside direction) releases are excellent for loud, dramatic cut-offs, but a more circular loop (inside or outside) is better for a gentle release.

Variable dynamics. Some pieces and movements end in a fermata accompanied by signs indicating variation in loudness over the duration of the hold. Three kinds of changes are possible—*crescendo, diminuendo,* or *crescendo e diminuendo.* These fermatas are entered in a usual manner but, instead of stopping at a hold position for the duration, some form of movement will continue during the hold and into the release loop. Ascending and outward movement communicates *crescendo*; descending and inward motion suggests *diminuendo.* Figure 5–17 presents some types of gestures that can be used to represent variable dynamics during a hold. Both hands can be employed effectively in these gestures.

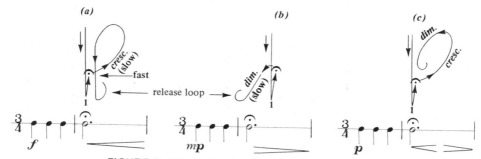

FIGURE 5–17. Fermatas with Variable Dynamics

Musical examples for study and practice. Musical Example 5–20 has a concluding fermata at a fixed dynamic, and Example 5–21 has one with a *crescendo e diminuendo* effect. Practice conducting each excerpt.

1. Musical Example 5–20 ends in a fermata entered on a downbeat. A firm, stable hold position in the right hand, or both hands, followed by a large heavy release in a downbeat or vertical-elliptical form is appropriate for termination of this piece. The hold is only moderately long—because of the quick tempo and relative value of the dotted-half note—and probably needs no special left-hand gesture to maintain the *fortissimo* level.

MUSICAL EXAMPLE 5–20. **Mendelssohn, Elijah, No. 20, Thanks Be to God, final measures (Chorus).**

2. The conclusion of the movement quoted in Musical Example 5–21 is marked with fermata and *crescendo-diminuendo* signs. You should enter the fermata at a *pianissimo* level and, relative to that basic dynamic, apply a gesture patterned after Figure 5–17*c*.

MUSICAL EXAMPLE 5–21.   **Schubert, Symphony No. 8 in B Minor, Movement II, final measures.**

SIX

The Four-Beat Pattern

Your experiences thus far conducting in triple meter and a three-beat pattern have enabled you to acquire a significant amount of fundamental conducting skill and ability to communicate expressive musical values through disciplined technique. Recall at this time some of the important things you can already do. You can conduct in a manner that represents a range of dynamics, tempos, and styles of articulation. You can prepare phrase attacks and cue entrances. You can communicate contour and points of stress or relaxation in a phrase. You can control the release of sound and the execution of fermatas in various musical situations. You can activate your left hand to independently signal entrances, releases, and changes in dynamics. Expanding your experience into music in quadruple meter conducted in a four-beat pattern will be relatively easy, because the same kinds of techniques and musical responses are involved. No new techniques are introduced in this chapter, but you will find that time and practice are required to develop skill and confidence in applying what you have learned to do in a three-beat form to a four-beat pattern.

FORM AND STYLE

A four-beat pattern should be used to conduct music in which the governing tempo beat is felt in an accent grouping of four pulses per measure. Figure 6–1 lists frequently encountered meter signatures that would require a four-beat conducting pattern and their applied meanings.

Observation of the graphic form of a four-beat pattern illustrated in Figure 6–2 reveals that its movement involves all four possible directions—down, in, out, and back (to rebound up). Practice this pattern in various sizes and tempos until maintaining its form becomes an automatic response to thinking and feeling meter grouped in fours. You should become conscious of the fact that the downbeat on 1, movement to the outside on 3, and coming back to near home base on 4 feel in physical response similar to the three beats of a three-beat pattern. Only beat 2 moving laterally to the inside is new.

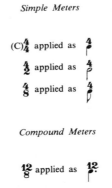

Simple Meters

(C)$\frac{4}{4}$ applied as

$\frac{4}{2}$ applied as

$\frac{4}{8}$ applied as

Compound Meters

$\frac{12}{8}$ applied as

FIGURE 6-1. Meters Applicable to a Four-beat Pattern

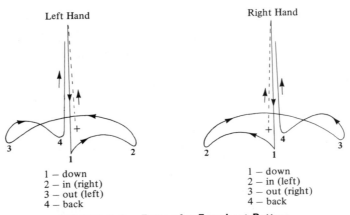

Left Hand

Right Hand

1 — down	1 — down
2 — in (right)	2 — in (left)
3 — out (left)	3 — out (right)
4 — back	4 — back

FIGURE 6-2. Form of a Four-beat Pattern

All of the physical elements introduced in Chapter Two and style characteristics in a beat pattern presented in Chapter Three are applicable to conducting in a four-beat pattern. You should renew your efforts to attain correct posture, hand position, and vertical and lateral movement. Figure 6-3 shows comparative forms for legato, *expressivo* legato, and marcato-staccato styles in a four-beat pattern. Review Figure 3-6 and related descriptions of movement in these styles of articulation before you practice each 4-beat style at various tempos and dynamic levels.

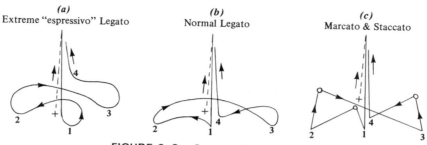

FIGURE 6-3. Comparative Styles

ON-BEAT ATTACKS

Preparation for on-beat attacks in a four-beat pattern requires essentially the same techniques as are used in a three-beat pattern. Preparatory motion for attacks on the first and final beats of a measure are the same in both patterns, and an attack on beat 3 (outside) in four-beat patterns compares with an attack on beat 2 in three-beat patterns. For this reason we will work first with attacks on beats 1, 3, and 4 followed by the new factor of attacks on beat 2 (inside).

Attacks on Beats 1, 3, and 4

You will recall from your work in Chapter Five that on-beat attacks can be classified as initial phrase attacks, subsequent phrase attacks, and internal attacks (points of stress) within a phrase. Figure 6-4 illustrates forms of preparation for initial attacks of a piece or movement starting on beat 3 or beat 4. It also shows enlarged preparatory motions that could be applied in a continuing beat pattern to communicate subsequent phrase attacks and internal attacks such as accents. (Preparation for attacks on beat 1, a downbeat, is the same in all beat patterns and needs no further graphic representation or verbal description.)

You should practice conducting each notated example in Figure 6-4 while

FIGURE 6-4. Preparation for Attacks on Beats 3 and 4

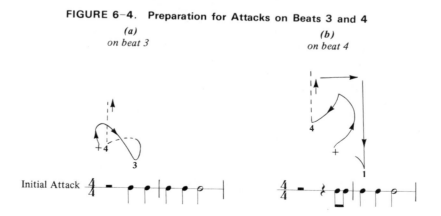

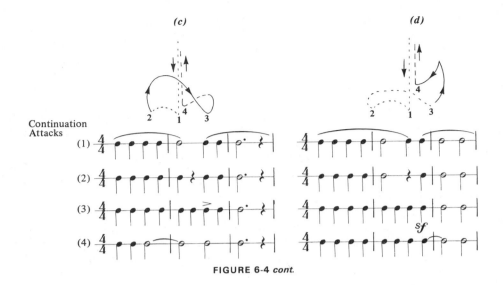

FIGURE 6-4 *cont.*

observing yourself in a mirror. Adjust the size of your preparatory motion and weight of the attack ictus to different styles, tempos, and dynamic levels. Try activating your left hand from time to time to give the attack gesture (Figure 4–3) as though it were an independent entrance cue or a reinforcement of the right-hand preparation for attack of an accented note.

Musical examples for study and practice. When you have achieved control of your conducting in a four-beat pattern so that you can communicate tempo, style, and on-beat attacks on beats 1, 3, and 4, go ahead to study and practice conducting Musical Examples 6–1 through 6–5.

1. Musical Example 6–1 has a quick tempo, *fortissimo* dynamic, and marcato style. Each of the two phrase attacks on a down-beat should have a preparatory motion that communicates these ongoing qualities. Set off your preparation for the attack of phrase 2 (beat 4, measure 4) by using a minibeat on the quarter rest and applying form *d* of Figure 6–4.

MUSICAL EXAMPLE 6–1. **Dvořák, Symphony No. 5 in E Minor** (*From* the New World), Movement IV, measures 18–25.

2. The lovely legato melody in Musical Example 6-2 is designed in four-measure phrases that start on beat 4. Use corresponding models from Figure 6–4 to prepare

your initial attack and each subsequent phrase attack. Continuation attack (*c3*) in Figure 6–4 will serve to communicate the *sforzando* on beat 3 in measure 12.

MUSICAL EXAMPLE 6–2. **Brahms, Symphony No. 1 in C Minor, Movement IV, measures 62–73 (Violin 1).**

3. The pronoun *I* (German, *ich*) in the text starts each phrase of the excerpt from a late Renaissance piece quoted in Musical Example 6–3. The beginning attack is on beat 3, but subsequent phrases start on beat 4 tied over to beat 1. These phrase attacks should not be done with accent or hard impact; rather they should have a light, clear attack followed by a little stretching (*crescendo*) of the sound into the next note. Illustrations in Figure 6–4 can be used again as models for your preparations, but you must adjust their size and weight to this music. Also, you should try to shape each phrase according to its contour.

MUSICAL EXAMPLE 6–3. **Hans Leo Hassler, edited by Herbert Zipper, I Leave Thee Love (Ich scheid von dir), beginning measures (Soprano 1).** Copyright 1952, by Broude Brothers. Used by permission.

4. Musical Example 6–4 is for double chorus (men and women). The opening one-measure motive starts on beat 3 with a *sforzando* attack and *diminuendo*. This motive is heard twice in the men's chorus and is restated in the women's chorus. With both hands raised high enough to be seen, direct your opening attack to the tenors and basses. Cue the soprano-alto entrance with an enlarged preparatory motion in the right hand (or both hands). Prepare each initial attack and each *sforzando* attack on beat 3 in the manner shown in Figure 6–4.

MUSICAL EXAMPLE 6–4. **Mendelssohn, Elijah, No. 11, Baal We Cry to Thee, beginning measures (Chorus).**

5. Eighth notes separated by eighth rests create a staccato style of articulation. Musical Example 6–5 should be conducted basically with a light, fast, staccato beat. Your pattern should be small, and your wrist should provide snap at each ictus. The *mezzo forte* half note introduces a point of stress which can be communicated with continuation-attack form (*c*3) in Figure 6–4.

MUSICAL EXAMPLE 6–5. **Tchaikovsky, The Nutcracker, March, beginning measures (Clarinet).**

Attacks on Beat 2 (Inside)

The ictus of the second beat in a four-beat pattern is to the inside of the ictus of the preceding downbeat. Preparatory motion for an on-beat attack to the inside must basically encompass the complete movement (full preparation) that would occur between the ictus points of the downbeat and beat 2. Figure 6–5 presents forms of preparation for initial attacks and continuation attacks that move inside to an ictus and rebound. A full preparatory motion for these attacks starts in the vicinity of home base for an initial attack and, literally, with the rebound from beat 1 if the attack occurs during a continuing beat pattern. You must make your rebound high enough from the preceding ictus, or home base, to permit your stroke into the attack ictus to move downward as well as inward. In heavy attacks

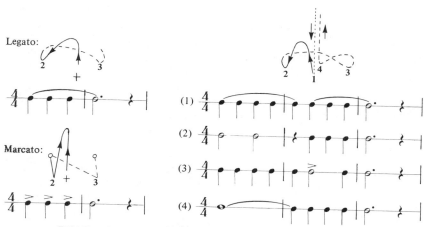

(a)
Initial Attacks

(b)
Continuation Attacks

FIGURE 6-5. Preparation for Attacks on Beat 2 (inside)

direction of the stroke might be mostly down. Your beat also must rebound from the attack ictus so as to follow a lateral movement to the outside to arrive at beat 3 in its normal location in the continuing four-beat pattern. Practice conducting each notated example in Figure 6–5.

It must be pointed out that there may be more than one correct way of doing something in conducting. There may be more than one acceptable option for handling a certain event in a piece of music. To help you develop your optimum skills, we have suggested specific techniques for you to apply in given situations, and in some, but not all, cases we have pointed out options.

Musical examples for study and practice. Musical Examples 6–6 through 6–8 include various situations that necessitate preparing phrase attacks or internal attacks on beat 2.

1. Musical Example 6–6 has an initial phrase attack on beat 2 for which you can prepare as shown in Figure 6–5a Legato. This attack is *piano* and in legato style. Shape the phrase according to its contour by gradually enlarging your legato beat pattern through the dotted-half note—so that no break will occur at this point in the phrase—and decrease and relax your beat as it moves to the cadence on the word *note*. Immediately after the ictus of beat 3, prepare for the second phrase attack on beat 4. (A phrasing release with the left hand could be used with the third beat of the cadence in phrase one.)

MUSICAL EXAMPLE 6-6. Orlando Gibbons, The Silver Swan, beginning measures (Soprano).

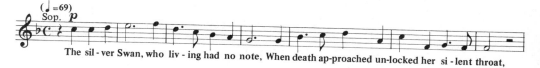

The sil - ver Swan, who liv - ing had no note, When death ap-proached un-locked her si - lent throat,

89

2. Both phrases in Musical Example 6–7 start in the chorus with a *forte* attack on beat 2. The accompaniment has an opening attack on beat 1, but otherwise it doubles the vocal parts, including silence at the quarter rest in measure 3. As you practice this excerpt, attend to the sequence of events described in the text and identified in the score by lettered arrows.

MUSICAL EXAMPLE 6–7.   Handel, The Messiah, No. 53, Worthy Is the Lamb That Was Slain, beginning measures (Chorus).

a. Prepare the opening downbeat attack in the accompaniment with your right hand.
b. Rebound high from the downbeat (Figure 6–5*b*) and activate the left hand to prepare in both hands the chorus entrance at a *forte* level on beat 2.
c. Sustain the cadence chord through beats 3 and 4 with the left hand extended high and somewhat forward, palm up. Turn the left hand into a forceful and quick release gesture at or just prior to the downbeat ictus at the rest.
d. Continue a full beat pattern in the right hand through the ictus of beat 4 preceding the rest. Move into the rest with a short downstroke, and rebound high to prepare the ensemble phrase attack on beat 2.
e. Prepare an attack for the on-beat syncopation in the soprano voice line in measure 6, beat 2. This internal point of stress can be communicated by either the right or left hand.

3. When you are conducting multiple voice lines, you must be aware of what is simultaneously happening in each line, not just of the general movement of the music. You must be able to give attention to one voice or a combination of voices, employing right- or left-hand gestures and eye contact to prepare attacks, shape phrases, and provide releases for one or more voices. Study Musical Example 6–8. You will observe that after all four voices have entered, horizontal pitch movement in an ascending conjunct (stepwise) progression starts in the bass line at measure 2, moves to soprano and alto lines in measure 4, then passes to the tenors and back to the sopranos. Bring these lines into the foreground of ensemble sound in the ways suggested in the sequence identified with lettered arrows.

a. The soprano opening attack (entrance) can be given primarily with a left-hand cue in conjunction with your right-hand beat.

b. Prepare the entrance of other parts with the right hand (Figure 6–4*c*) and raise the conducting base line for this preparation and ictus of beat 3 so it will be in view of all singers.

c. Direct eye contact, along with your preparation and downbeat, to the bass section as it starts a pattern of melodic interest.

d. Shift your attention to the sopranos (conductor's left) at the downbeat of measure 3 and activate your left hand to give them a preparatory gesture and attack for starting their pitch movement following a note of long duration.

e. Give the tenors attention similar to that just given the sopranos, except you can handle the preparation in your right hand, assuming the tenors are to the conductor's right.

f. Attention should come back to the sopranos for the same reason and in the same way stated at arrow *d* in the example.

g. Ensemble precision and unity in attacking final cadence chords is important. Within the soft, sustained nature of the ending, prepare clearly for the chord attacks on beats 1 and 3. Beats 2 and 4 are unimportant except for their relative duration; observe them with minibeats.

h. You should conduct through the final measure because the instrumental accompaniment enters again at this point and extends the ending through two more measures. Use a left-hand release loop (Figure 5–4) with beat 4 for the choir's final release.

MUSICAL EXAMPLE 6–8. **Mendelssohn, Elijah, No. 29, He, Watching Over Israel, final measures (Chorus).**

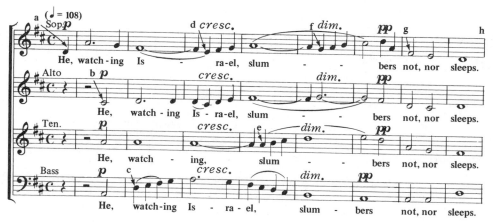

RELEASES

You now must learn to apply the forms of release gestures described and practiced in Chapter Five to musical situations in the four-beat pattern. Right-hand releases on the first and last beats can be handled in the same ways used on the first and last beats of a three-beat pattern. A cut-off on beat 2 (inside) involves a new experience, and one on beat 3 (outside) needs some modification of the similar situation on beat 2 (outside) in triple meter. You also can activate your left hand to give a release gesture at any point in a four-beat pattern. Releases on beats 2 and 3 are presented here in the categories of final releases and continuation releases.

Final Releases on Beats 2 and 3

Conducting movement ceases at the end of a release gesture concluding a piece or movement. No concern exists for being in a position to continue in the beat pattern; hence, any of the forms of release gesture shown in Figure 6–6 can be applied. Your choice should be based on personal preference and which form integrates best with the aesthetic and dramatic effects of the musical ending. Right-hand movements are pictured; left-hand motions would reverse left and right directions when used to duplicate and reinforce the right hand in a final cut-off.

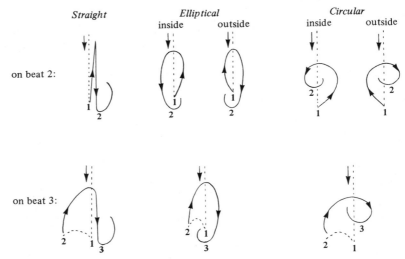

FIGURE 6–6.   Forms of Final Release on Beats 2 and 3

Continuation Releases on Beats 2 and 3

Releases during a piece of music occur in situations that require continuation of the beat pattern following a phrasing or an interruption such as a caesura or rest. In all such cases you should be in a position at the end of the release loop to stroke into the next ictus in the beat pattern. Remember, too, that beats during rests are sometimes negated or done as minibeats (review Figure 5–8). Figure 6–7 illustrates release loops substituted for each beat of a four-beat pattern plus a left-hand release gesture that can be applied on any beat. First practice the right-hand patterns alone, then practice activating your left hand for the primary release on each beat. Your left-hand gesture, when used as a primary release signal, should

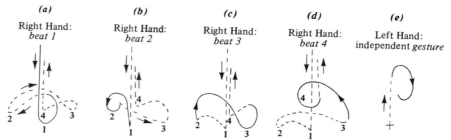

FIGURE 6-7. Forms of Continuation Releases in a Four-beat Pattern

be given at a level higher than the right-hand beat pattern and directed, along with eye contact, to the section or sections of the ensemble making the release.

Musical Examples for Study and Practice. Musical Examples 6–9 through 6–13 include both final releases and continuation releases within a four-beat pattern. Study each example and become acquainted with the sound of it. Practice conducting the excerpts, employing the suggested techniques, until you believe you have musical control throughout your conducting. You will find opportunities to apply releases with the right hand alone, the left hand independently, and both hands together.

1. Musical Example 6–9 starts with two one-measure motives punctuated by an eighth rest occupying the last half of beat 4. You can communicate this phrasing with a left-hand gesture on count 4. Prepare, after the ictus of beat 4 in measure 2, for a *fortissimo* attack on the downbeat of measure 3 and continue slowing the tempo into the final three chords. These chords are very slow and heavily accented. You can conduct the first two with heavy downbeats and come into the final chord with a large elliptical or circular release loop in both hands. Your follow-through should be long and slow in order to fill the beat's duration.

MUSICAL EXAMPLE 6–9. Bizet, L'Arlésienne Suite No. 2, Intermezzo, final measures.

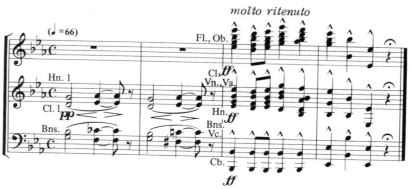

2. Substitute a release loop for beat 4 (Figure 6–7d) in your right-hand pattern in the first measure of Musical Example 6–10. This release should be heavy (*fortissimo*) and quick, representing only an eighth-note duration. Activate

your left hand into a *subito pianissimo* gesture during the eighth rest to prepare the *pianissimo* attack. Chord punctuations represented by eighth rests in the next to final measure can be communicated with a very light staccato beat on counts 2 and 4. Use a circular form of release loop (Figure 6–6) for the final release on beat 3 in the last measure. Your follow-through should occupy the beat's entire duration.

MUSICAL EXAMPLE 6–10. **Fritz Velke, Concertino for Band, Movement II, final measures (condensed score).** ©MCMLXII, Templeton Publishing Co., Inc., Sole Selling Agent: Shawnee Press, Inc., Delaware Water Gap, Pa. 18327. Used by permission.

3. The chorus in Musical Example 6–11 releases an eighth note on the first half of beat 3 in each of the first two measures. The accompaniment continues on count 4 in measure 1, but all voices are silent on count 4 in measure 2. Try a left-hand phrasing gesture to the chorus in measure 1, followed by right-hand attacks on beat 4 (instrumental accompaniment) and beat 1 (chorus, measure 2). Release all voices with a two-hand loop on beat 3 (measure 2), negate beat 4, and prepare with your right hand for a *forte* attack in all parts on the next downbeat. Activate your left hand in a *diminuendo* gesture at approximately beat 2 of the next to final measure. Continue the *diminuendo* gesture, along with decreasing the size and weight of your right-hand beat, and end with a gentle release loop in both hands on beat 3. Your follow-through should be timed to represent an eighth-note value.

MUSICAL EXAMPLE 6–11. **Gounod, Messe Solennelle, No. II, Gloria in Excelsis.**

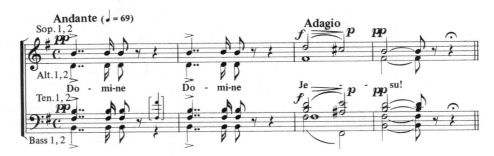

4. Continuation releases are a significant factor in conducting Musical Example 6–12. Repetitions of the snare drum rhythm pattern need no particular attention, so concentrate on the cornet-trumpet line, which you can conduct quite effectively with only your right hand. Strong downbeat attacks are important

in the first two measures. In measure 3 terminate the downbeat with a snappy release loop, negate beat 2, and prepare an accented attack on beat 3. Continue with strong downbeat attacks in measures 4 and 5, insert a quick (staccato) release loop for beat 2 (Figure 6–7*b*) in measure 5, negate beat 3 and prepare the attack on beat 4. Practice this excerpt until you can quickly anticipate preparing attacks and inserting release loops. You might find chanting the voice line with "tah" will help you to conduct it with greater confidence.

MUSICAL EXAMPLE 6–12. **Vaclav Nelhybel, Trittico, No. I, measures 9–15 (condensed score).** ©Copyright 1965 by Franco Colombo, Inc. Used by permission.

5. Attend the phrasing in all voice parts in Musical Example 6–13 by activating your left hand to give an independent phrasing release (Figure 6–7*e*) with beat 4, measure 2. The gesture should fill at least the first half of count 4, permitting a musical punctuation and breath on the remainder of the count's duration.

MUSICAL EXAMPLE 6–13. **Mendelssohn, Elijah, No. 32, He That Shall Endure, beginning measures (Chorus).**

FERMATAS

In Chapter Five you learned fundamental techniques for conducting fermatas from the standpoints of entering them on any beat of a three-beat pattern and leaving them under various musical conditions. Review Figures 5–11 through 5–17 before continuing.

Fermatas, you will recall, can occur at the end of a piece or during the course of a piece. Concluding holds are more common than continuation holds. As a matter of fact, fermatas in the midst of a piece are uncommon except in chorales, where most of them are not even treated as holds. They are found with more frequency in late eighteenth- and nineteenth-century music (such as Beethoven), but twentieth-century composers have been more inclined to notate exact durations and not leave the length of hold to the discretion of performers. Nevertheless, you must be able to conduct fermatas when you encounter them. Figures 6–8 through 6–10 include a variety of conditions for entering and leaving fermatas

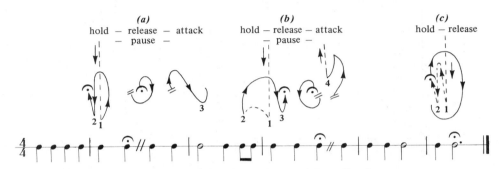

FIGURE 6–8.   Fermatas Followed by a Break

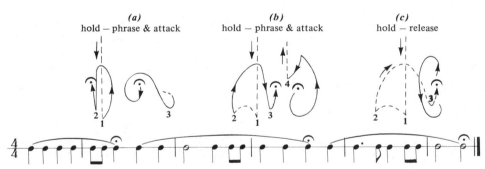

FIGURE 6–9.   Fermatas Followed by a Phrasing Interruption

FIGURE 6–10.   Fermatas Followed by No Interruption

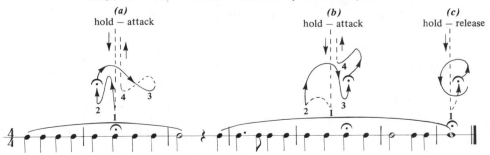

within a four-beat pattern. Study the drawings of movements for each situation and conduct the nonpitch exercises until you have control of the techniques involved. Practice with your right hand alone and with your left hand activated to function with the right in entering and leaving the holds.

Musical Examples for Study and Practice

1. Musical Example 6–14 is strongly accented, slow and broad, and as loud as possible within an acceptable musical tone. Prepare the phrase attack on beat 2 with these qualities in mind. You should have a large preparatory motion leading to the attack of each half note (beats 1 and 3); therfore, relatively decrease your motion into beats 2 and 4. The final fermata in all chorus parts is entered on beat 2. Both this note and the preceding note on beat 1 can be attacked with long, heavy downbeats similar to the final measure in Figure 6–8. A left-hand gesture for more sound (Figure 4–9) sustained, with vibration in the forearm and hand, through the fermata would be an excellent option for this dynamic ending. Either a straight or vertical-elliptical form of release in both hands will maintain a high level of energy into the cut-off.

MUSICAL EXAMPLE 6–14. **Flor Peeters, Jubilate Deo Omnis Terra, SATB.** Copyright ©1954 by McLaughlin & Reilly Company. Used by permission. All rights reserved.

2. The fermata on beat 3 in Musical Example 6–15 is entered in marcato style and left with a phrasing release and an attack on beat 4 directed to the entire ensemble for the start of a repetition of the motive. Figure 6–9*b* shows a similar situation, but adjust your movement for the sound of this music (a quick marcato release and attack). An eighth rest and attack after the beat follow the second fermata and are omitted from this excerpt because such a situation involves a new technique that will be introduced in Chapter Eight.

MUSICAL EXAMPLE 6–15. **Schumann, Symphony No. 1 in B Flat Major (Spring), beginning measures.**

3. Musical Example 6–16 is for chorus and instrumental accompaniment. First, look at the instrumental part under the choir's fermata. You must keep your right-hand beat into the fourth count, which can be a staccato beat followed by an arrest until time to prepare the next phrase attack. Use your left hand to enter, hold, and release the fermata in the vocal parts. This release should be only a phrasing loop that rebounds into preparation (joined by the right hand) for the next downbeat attack.

MUSICAL EXAMPLE 6–16. **Haydn, The Creation, No. 11, Awake the Harp, measures 46–48.**

4. Direct your downbeat attack of the opening fermata in Musical Example 6–17 to the horns. Think through four tempo beats, and slightly more, to make certain you have held the note as a fermata. Give a gentle phrasing release and continue without pause into the next downbeat attack directed toward the low strings. Your continuing beat should be in staccato style to represent *pizzicato* articulation in the theme. Accents marked in the score can be prepared within your right-hand beat pattern.

MUSICAL EXAMPLE 6–17. Grieg, Peer Gynt Suite No. 1, No. IV (In the Hall of the Mountain-King), beginning measures.

Two-Beat and One-Beat Patterns

Thus far you have had experiences with conducting music using three-beat and four-beat patterns. There is a large quantity and variety of music in triple and quadruple meters and, unless you conduct a lot of marches, you will be using these two conducting patterns more than any others over your future years. Working with three-beat and four-beat patterns has enabled you to develop skills of movement in all possible directions, abilities to prepare attacks and releases with either hand, and capacities to communicate expressive values in the music. In this chapter we will study two-beat and one-beat conducting patterns. Because you already possess a great deal of fundamental technique and knowledge that can be transferred to the new patterns, both can be introduced in rather close succession. Your progress beyond the introductory level will require continued practice in applying your knowledge and skill to a variety of situations in musical scores.

TWO-BEAT PATTERNS

A two-beat pattern should be used to conduct music in which the governing tempo beat is felt in an accent grouping of two pulses per measure. Figure 7–1 lists the most frequently encountered meter signatures and their applied meanings that would lead to a decision to conduct in two beats.

Form and Style

The two-beat pattern, in a manner of speaking, has only a first and a last beat. These two beats correspond in many ways to the first and last beats of other

Simple Meters

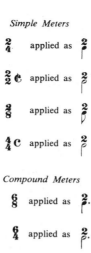

Compound Meters

FIGURE 7–1. Meters Applicable to a Two-Beat Pattern

patterns. Beat 1 is the same kind of downbeat, and the ictus of beat 2 is back to the vicinity of the first ictus (or home-base position). Traditional forms and comparative styles are shown in Figure 7–2. Normal legato form has soft ictus points and a slightly curved line of movement between them. Extreme legato has a curved ictus on each beat. Marcato-staccato style is characterized by sharp ictus points and angular rebounds with an arrest (stop) at the top of each. Figure 7–2 also shows an optional staccato form, especially functional at a very fast tempo. Its rebound from beat 1 is very short and the stroke (done with a snap of the wrist) into beat 2 travels a short distance downward into an ictus at essentially the same place as that for the downbeat. Practice only the normal legato and marcato-staccato forms at various tempos and dynamic levels until you have a two-beat pattern that is controlled and pleasing to the sight.

An experienced conductor from time to time varies the form of any basic beat pattern in making adjustments to the expressive nature of the music. Perhaps the two-beat pattern has more acceptable modifications than others. Two of these alterations along with their functional applications are presented in Figure 7–3.

Some beginning students in conducting have problems demonstrating a two-beat pattern that has correct form, clarity, and smoothly coordinated movement.

FIGURE 7–2. Two-Beat Form, Comparative Styles

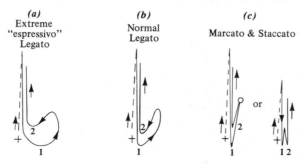

| *(a)* Extreme "espressivo" Legato | *(b)* Normal Legato | *(c)* Marcato & Staccato |

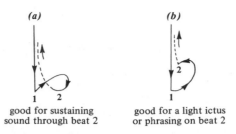

good for sustaining   good for a light ictus
sound through beat 2   or phrasing on beat 2

FIGURE 7–3. Variations in the Two-Beat Form

One of the most helpful suggestions is to avoid incorrect forms of the kind illustrated in Figure 7–4. Form *a* has a downbeat that slides far to the outside and never strokes downward into a clear ictus; beat 2 retraces the vague route of beat 1. Form *b* is a roller coaster in which the perpetual down–up motion has no clear ictus and no identification of a primary downbeat. Badly formed beat patterns such as these cannot function to communicate either ensemble precision or musical expression.

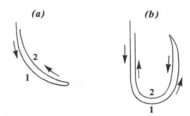

FIGURE 7–4. Incorrect Forms of a Two-Beat Pattern

Attacks, Releases, and Fermatas

Techniques for communicating on-beat attacks, releases, and fermatas in a two-beat pattern are essentially the same as those used on the first and last beats of other patterns. Phrase attacks and internal attacks, release loops, and entrances to fermatas on beat 1 are applied to the downbeat. Similar events on beat 2 have a preparatory motion that starts with a higher than usual rebound from the ictus of beat 1 and continues to stroke or loop downward and inward toward the ictus of beat 2.

To help you develop skill in conducting duple meter, two types of practice material are provided here. You should first work with the nonpitch exercises, which show how to apply specific techniques. When you gain confidence in your technique, go on to the examples from music literature.

Nonpitch exercises for study and practice. Each of the following eight-measure exercises has two phrases, a beat unit and metronome marking, and fixed dynamic markings. Some contain accents and fermatas, and all provide graphic illustrations suggesting movements to handle important things such as initial attacks on beat 2, phrase releases and attacks, accents, and fermata entrances and releases. Practice these exercises, giving attention to the details they include and to the form of your basic beat pattern.

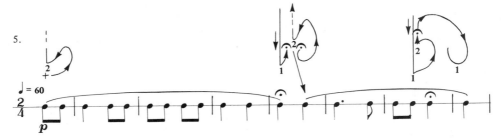

5.

Musical examples for study and practice. Musical Examples 7–1 through 7–7 provide opportunities to apply conducting techniques you have mastered in three-beat and four-beat patterns to similar musical situations in a two-beat pattern. Play or sing each excerpt, or listen to a recording if one is available, to become acquainted with its sound, for your success in conducting depends to a large extent on a complete aural concept of the music.

1. Musical Example 7–1 has a sustained pedal tone in horns and cellos starting two measures before the thematic material (Violin 1), which is designed in the form of a musical sentence comprised of two four-measure phrases. The tempo is quick, the dynamics are soft, and the style is a mixture of light legato and staccato. Direct your initial attack to horns and cellos, and cue the violin entrance with eye contact plus a left-hand attack gesture. Enlarge your preparatory motion for the downbeat attack of phrase two.

MUSICAL EXAMPLE 7–1. **Haydn, Symphony No. 104 in D Major, Movement IV, beginning measures.**

Allegro spiritoso (♩ =138)

2. Prepare the initial attack on beat 2 in Musical Example 7–2 as illustrated in nonpitch exercises numbers 2 and 5 above. Your preparatory motion must communicate the quick tempo and light staccato attacks at the beginning. Try each of the forms for a marcato-staccato style shown in Figure 7–2 and decide which you prefer for this music. Repeat the theme as written and give a good preparation for the repeated phrase attack on beat 2 (see nonpitch exercise 2).

MUSICAL EXAMPLE 7–2. **Haydn, Symphony No. 88 in G Major, Movement IV, beginning measures (Violin 1).**

Allegro con spirito(♩ =144)

3. Musical Example 7–3 has a meter signature of four-four, but tempo indications leave no doubt that a half-note functions as the beat unit and the music must be conducted with a two-beat pattern. Your main responsibility is to communicate dynamic changes and control attacks and releases. Build the *crescendo* in your right-hand beat, bring it into a large release loop on beat 2, measure 4, and continue to a *forte* attack on the next downbeat (review a similar situation of phrase release-attack illustrated in nonpitch exercise 3). Communicate the *piano* attack, measure 6, by reducing size and weight in your right-hand beat immediately following the ictus of beat 2, measure 5, and simultaneously activating your left hand in a *subito-piano* gesture (Figure 4–8). Release the final measure with a phrasing release (both hands) occupying all of beat 2.

MUSICAL EXAMPLE 7–3. **Mendelssohn, Elijah, No. 10, As God the Lord of Sabaoth, measures 78–84 (Chorus).**

4. Practice an *expressivo* legato style of beat (Figure 7–2*a*) in Musical Example 7–4. Shape each of the two phrases according to its dynamic markings and give a left-hand phrasing release (nonpitch exercise 2) with beat 1 in measure 4. Timing for attack of the first note of phrase two—the pick-up eighth in measure 4—will occur correctly if you give a full preparatory motion for the downbeat of measure 5.

MUSICAL EXAMPLE 7–4. **Liszt, Les Préludes, measures 260–267 (Violin 1 and 2).**

5. A major period of silence separates *fortissimo* and *piano* sections in the condensed band score quoted in Musical Example 7–5. You should try to reflect in your conducting what the music does in sound and silence. Conduct the first three measures with a very fast and heavy marcato beat ending in a large release loop, substituted for beat 2 of measure 3, to signal an abrupt cessation of all sound. Continue without break or arrest into minibeats in the light staccato form shown in Figure 7–2 and keep these through the two measures of rest. Take no action

during the silence that will suggest response from the players until you rebound from the ictus on the final beat of rest and enlarge your preparatory motion crossing the bar line into the *piano* attack. Adding the left hand to either the release or attack gestures can be done at your option.

MUSICAL EXAMPLE 7–5. **Donald H. White, Patterns for Band, measures 112–116 (condensed score).** ©Copyright 1969 by Elkan-Vogel Co., Inc. Used by permission.

6. Musical Example 7–6 is in compound meter conducted in two beats per measure. The lettered arrows will help you quickly identify places in the score where fermatas can be controlled in ways described here.

- a. Enter the first fermata on a downbeat and hold it beyond two tempo beats. Leave this hold position without interruption and move with a large preparatory motion into a downbeat attack of the second fermata.
- b. Hold the second fermata and leave it with a phrasing release, which must continue as preparation for a *fortissimo* downbeat attack in instrumental parts followed immediately with a preparation and cue (add the left hand) for attack by the male voices on beat 2.
- c. Handle this fermata in the same way as the first.
- d. From the preceding fermata, enter the last one with a downbeat and hold it beyond one count's duration. If you respond to the exact way it is written, you will give this fermata a complete release (use any form you feel to be appropriate). Continue by thinking the ictus of beat 2 (rest) in tempo and moving immediately with full preparation for the next downbeat attack.

MUSICAL EXAMPLE 7–6. **Mendelssohn, Elijah, No. 13, Call Him Louder, measures 65–76 (Chorus).**

7. The first fermata in Musical Example 7–7 occurs in the midst of a phrase and should be left without a release (a review of Figure 6–10 will help you recall this technique). Treat the second fermata as a phrase ending and give it a *forte* phrasing release. Apply an immediate brake action to your follow-through in order to cross the bar line with a short stroke into a *pianissimo* attack and, at the same time, activate your left hand in a *subito-pianissimo* gesture.

MUSICAL EXAMPLE 7–7. Mendelssohn, Elijah, No. 34, Behold, God the Lord, beginning measures (Chorus).

ONE-BEAT PATTERNS

There are musical situations where only one conducting beat per measure can be maintained effectively. Meter signatures in music conducted in one-beat patterns are ordinarily either duple or triple meter. Whether to conduct in two or three beats or in one beat is determined by the tempo and the kind of note that functions best as the beat unit at that tempo. In very fast tempos the performer usually feels only one underlying pulse governing the flow of durations through each measure; therefore, only one conducting beat should be used to represent this basic tempo beat. Decisions to conduct in one-beat patterns are based on indications in the score such as metronome markings, tempo terms, or the genre of the piece (for example, scherzo, valse). Some pieces or major sections require one-beat patterns throughout, but in twentieth-century music a common condition is to find only one or a few one-beat measures among other meters in a rhythmic organization based on changing meters (Chapter Eleven). Figure 7–5 presents typical meter signatures, their applied meanings that result in a one-beat conducting pattern, and indications of their relative frequency in music literature.

FIGURE 7–5. Meters Conducted with a One-Beat Pattern

Meter Signature	Applied Meaning	Frequency
$\frac{1}{4}$	♩	very infrequent
$\frac{2}{4}$	♩	occasionally—at a very fast tempo in either traditional or contemporary music
$\frac{3}{4}$	♩.	fairly common—at very fast tempos in either traditional or contemporary music
$\frac{2}{8}$	♪	occasionally—in fast tempos and changing meters in contemporary music
$\frac{3}{8}$	♪.	fairly common—in fast tempos and changing meters in contemporary music

Form and Style

A one-beat pattern theoretically consists of a straight downward stroke and a straight upward rebound for every measure. This form can create problems for singers and players, because successive downbeats over a period of time might begin to appear all the same. Straight down and up movements also are more mechanical and limit a conductor's creative and expressive communication. For these reasons the one-beat pattern takes various functional forms shown in Figure 7-6.

Form *a* in Figure 7-6 is a standard one-beat pattern acceptable for use in most situations. Continuation of a straight beat over long periods can become monotonous unless movement is varied by alternation with one or more of the other forms. A natural alternative is form *b*, which adapts particularly well to light staccato articulations. Ictus points in this form move back and forth laterally (right-left) on each successive measure. Form *c*, because of its whiplike action, is the most forceful of options for a one-beat pattern; it adapts well to an accented (marcato) style of beat. Form *d* has a smooth flow of movement and a slightly rounded ictus, representative of sustained sound or legato articulation.

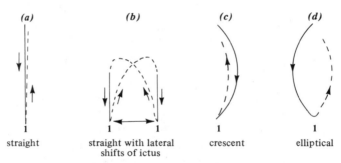

FIGURE 7-6. Forms of One-Beat Patterns

Phrasal Grouping of Measures

Another artistic solution to problems caused by repetitive one-beat patterns can sometimes be found in a phrasal grouping of measures and beats. When music progresses in clearly definable phrases or subphrases, measures can be combined into a beat pattern corresponding to the number of measures in the unit. Thus, a three-measure phrase is conducted in a three-beat pattern, a four-measure phrase in a four-beat pattern, and so forth. The fact that some measures have no downbeat is not confusing under these circumstances. Phrasal conducting should be used when it will contribute better communication of an expressive phrase line (see Musical Example 7-11).

Attacks, Releases, and Fermatas

On-beat attacks, releases, and fermatas in a one-beat pattern occur on a downbeat and are handled like downbeats of other conducting patterns. The continuation of movement following one of these events is to another downbeat in the next measure. The same situations encountered during phrasal groupings are executed within the beat pattern being used at the time.

Nonpitch exercises for study and practice. Exercises 1 to 4 include elements that require applications of techniques for controlling attacks, releases, and fermatas. Practice each until you feel comfortable with your techniques and with the basic styles and forms of a one-beat pattern.

1. Form *a* – Figure 7–6, legato style

2. Form *b* – Figure 7–6, staccato style

3. Form *d* – Figure 7–6, legato style

4. Form *c* for phrase 1, phrasal grouping for phrase 2

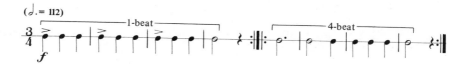

1. Musical Example 7–8 is a variation in duple meter of the movement's opening theme in triple meter quoted in Musical Example 3–6 (compare the two). Tempo markings and meter signature provide information for making the decision to conduct this section in half-note beats, or one beat per measure; quarter-note beats at the rate of 184 per minute are too rapid to be clear and precise. Either form *a* or *b* in Figure 7–6 could be used to conduct this soft, staccato excerpt.

MUSICAL EXAMPLE 7–8. **Brahms, Symphony No. 2 in D Major, Movement III, measures 33–40 (Violin 1).**

2. Observe in Musical Example 7–9 that the soprano line divides into four-measure melodic phrases that would conduct nicely in four-beat phrasal groupings, except for the fact that the other three parts moving in parallel triads (first inversions) start a measure later in canon fashion and do not fit the same phrasal grouping. Your best choice is to use one-beat patterns throughout this short piece. A crescent form could be used to represent the *forte* accented style. You can give the opening attack to sopranos and cue other entrances a measure later with eye contact plus addition of a left-hand preparation for measure 2.

3. Changes from other patterns to a one-beat pattern, or conversely from one-beat patterns to other patterns, sometimes are necessary during the course of a piece or movement. Such a circumstance arises in Musical Example 7–10 (found later in the same movement from which examples 3–5 and 7–8 were quoted). You can attend to important musical events in this excerpt by applying techniques suggested relevant to the lettered arrows.

a. Conduct in a three-beat pattern at the tempo given.

b. Shift your attention to passing of the theme to the oboes, continue a *diminuendo*, and introduce a *ritardando*.

c. Give a left-hand phrasing release with beat 3 and cross the double bar with a right-hand preparation for your downbeat attack, one-beat pattern, and new tempo.

d. Use form *a*, Figure 7–6, during at least the first four measures. The straight one-beat form is clear and precise; therefore, it is useful to start a change from another beat pattern.

e. You could vary your beat form with the change of rhythmic motive. Interesting options would be either a one-beat pattern, form *b*, or two-measure groupings conducted in a two-beat pattern. Remember to cue the flute entrance.

MUSICAL EXAMPLE 7–9. Randall Thompson, Mass of the Holy Spirit, Hosanna, opening measures. ©Copyright 1956, by E. C. Schirmer Music Co., Boston. Used by permission.

MUSICAL EXAMPLE 7–10. Brahms, Symphony No. 2 in D Major, Movement III, measures 121–135 (Violin 1, Oboes, Flute 1).

4. Musical Example 7–11 offers an excellent opportunity to use four-beat phrasal groupings in the second theme. Start with a light staccato beat in either form *a* or *b*. In measure 9 give a glance to the individual playing the violin solo part, enlarge your preparatory motion to communicate a change to *forte* level, and move into a downbeat (measure 10), which becomes beat 1 of a four-beat pattern in legato style.

MUSICAL EXAMPLE 7–11. **Saint-Saens, Danse Macabre, measures 41–57 (Violin 1, Violin Solo).**

EIGHT

After-Beat Attacks, Accents, and Syncopations

You have become aware, during your study of chapters four through seven, of the conductor's responsibilities in preparing an ensemble's voice parts for attacks at the right time and in correct ways, according to the musical score. Experiences so far have been with on-beat attacks, which occur at the beginning of a beat's duration and at an ictus point in the beat pattern. The techniques studied have been those necessary to communicate attacks at the beginnings of phrases or motives and at certain points of stress within a phrase. Many other important attacks in music happen after a beat—following an ictus, yet at some point within that beat's duration. In this chapter you will study and practice after-beat attacks (initial and internal) as well as off-beat accents and syncopations. Preparation for these kinds of attacks requires new techniques.

AFTER-BEAT ATTACKS

Points in Time

Points within a count's duration at which most after-beat attacks take place can be generally classified into three types as shown in Figure 8-1. We will use the term *off-beat* in reference to the exact midpoint of a count's duration in simple meters (it is not applicable, ordinarily, in compound meters). Many attacks and accents occur squarely on the off-beat; others precede or follow this point.

Form of the Preparatory Motion

Off-beat attacks are the easiest and most practical to try first. The fundamental technique for communicating an off-beat attack is based on the kind of preparatory

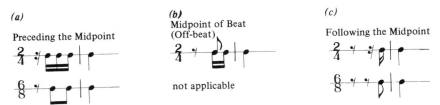

FIGURE 8-1. Points in Time for After-Beat Attacks

motion employed. We will call this motion a *half preparation* because it uses about one-half of the movement and time required in a *full preparation*, which, you will recall, signals an on-beat attack. (Some authors use the term *unprepared beat*, but, of course, an after-beat attack does have preparation, so *unprepared* may be less descriptive than *half preparation*.)

Figure 8-2 compares the forms of preparatory gestures for on-beat and off-beat attacks related to an outside ictus (beat 2 in three, or beat 3 in four). A full preparation includes the complete continuous movement from the preceding ictus, or preparatory position, and consists of the combined duration of rebound and stroke components. The timing provided by a full preparation creates both a physical and a psychological communication for an on-beat response. The form of a half preparation, on the other hand, is made up of only a stroke directly into the ictus after which an attack occurs. A clearly marked ictus point is important, for it is this element that enables exact timing of an off-beat attack by members of an ensemble.

FIGURE 8-2. Comparative Preparatory Motions

Initial and Continuation Off-Beat Attacks

Off-beat attacks, as well as on-beat attacks, can occur at the start of a piece or movement; they can be found as attacks of subsequent phrases or motives during a piece; and they can appear within phrases in circumstances such as the continuation of pitch and rhythmic movement following a rest or a note of long duration. We will refer to an attack at the beginning of a piece or movement as an *initial attack* and use the term *continuation attack* for any of those involved with subsequent phrases. The technique for conducting initial attacks requires executing a half preparation from the ready stance; subsequent off-beat attacks are prepared within a continuing beat pattern. Your concept of how and when to prepare for off-beat attacks will solidify as you study descriptions of the elements of movement and their graphic illustrations in Figures 8-3 through 8-6.

Execution of initial off-beat attacks. A beginning off-beat attack can be communicated successfully if you follow these patterns of movement: (1) Assume a preparatory stance (ready position) in which your hand is at a point farthest away from the ictus into which the stroke will move. This position is approximately the top of a rebound from an imaginary preceding ictus. (2) Stroke directly into the ictus point. Avoid moving farther away (in an opposite direction), since players or singers may confuse such a movement with a full preparation for an on-beat attack. The opening tempo, dynamic level, and style can be communicated in a half preparation as well as in a full preparation. (3) Rebound firmly and clearly from the ictus, feel the off-beat attack of sound coinciding with the top of your rebound (Figure 8–2*b*), and then continue in a normal beat pattern.

Execution of continuation off-beat attacks. Performance of off-beat attacks during the course of a piece should follow these guidelines: (1) Create an arrest (stop) at the end of a small rebound from the preceding ictus. This causes a momentary delay before the following stroke. (2) Stroke directly—in a straight line—into the ictus after which the off-beat attack takes place. This stroke is somewhat faster than usual to compensate for the arrest, to arrive at the ictus in tempo, and to stimulate an off-beat response. (3) Feel the off-beat attack of sound at the top of the rebound portion of your continuing beat pattern.

Figures 8–3 to 8–6 show forms of preparation for communicating both initial and continuation off-beat attacks after every beat in a four-beat pattern; thus every direction used in conducting is represented. Half preparations in other beat patterns copy those of corresponding direction (that is, down, out, in, or back) from a four-beat pattern. You should practice conducting each notated example in all four figures to acquire the techniques of executing half preparations in various contexts.

You can activate your left hand to cue off-beat attacks independently or to reinforce right-hand preparations in selected situations. Figure 8–7 shows two forms, one of which should be applicable to any beat of a conducting pattern. Practice again the notated examples in Figures 8–3 to 8–6, and this time activate

FIGURE 8–3. **Preparation for Off-Beat Attacks after a Downbeat**

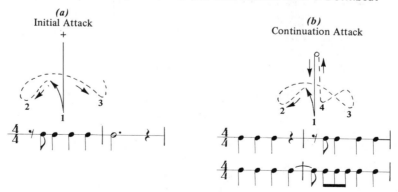

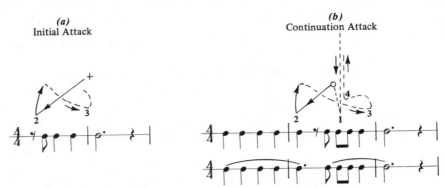

FIGURE 8-4. Preparation for Off-Beat Attacks after a Beat to the Inside

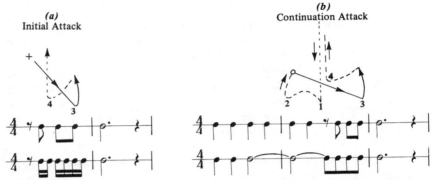

FIGURE 8-5. Preparation for Off-Beat Attacks after a Beat to the Outside

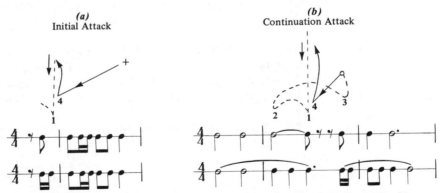

FIGURE 8-6. Preparation for Off-Beat Attacks after the Last Beat of a Measure

FIGURE 8-7. Left-Hand Preparations for Off-Beat Attacks

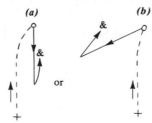

your left hand to give the primary preparation for off-beat attacks. Form *b*, Figure 8–7, will work well to the outside and form *a* will coordinate easily at all other points of the right-hand pattern.

Musical examples for study and practice. Musical Examples 8–1 through 8–5 contain both initial and continuation off-beat attacks for a variety of musical situations. Study each written excerpt, learn how it sounds, and practice conducting it while incorporating techniques suggested in relation to points identified by lettered arrows.

    1. Conduct Musical Example 8–1 with a light staccato two-beat pattern at the quick tempo indicated.

        a. Apply a preparatory motion like the one in Figure 8–6*a* for your initial attack.

        b. Use a similar half preparation on beat 2 of your continuing beat in order to communicate a clear attack of phrase 2.

MUSICAL EXAMPLE 8–1. **Haydn, Symphony No. 94 in G Major (Surprise), Movement IV, beginning measures (Violin 1).**

    2. Musical Example 8–2 has both off-beat and on-beat attacks at important places in its phrase structure. This well-known Romantic theme moves at a moderately slow tempo, in legato style, and with variable dynamics throughout.

        a. Employ the form of initial attack shown in Figure 8–5*a*.

        b. A phrase repetition starts after beat 3; use the continuation form of off-beat attack in Figure 8–5*b* and adapt it to your feeling for this music.

        c. You must build to a climax by continuing without a phrase break through the *crescendo* between counts 1 and 3. Enlarge your beat pattern during count 2 and move with a full preparation into the *forte* attack on beat 3.

        d. Another stress comes on beat 3, measure 5. Relax your beat on count 2 and continue with an enlarged full preparation into count 3.

        e. Repetitions occur from this point on in the theme; apply techniques of the kind used in the first six measures.

MUSICAL EXAMPLE 8–2. **Tchaikovsky, Symphony No. 6 in B Minor (Pathetique), Movement I, measures 89–100 (Violin 1).**

3. Chorus parts only are quoted in Musical Example 8−3 because they alone provide an excellent opportunity to practice off-beat attacks. The first ones occur after the downbeat in three consecutive measures—an unusual situation.

    a. Chorus and instruments have the same opening attack; use the form of initial off-beat attack shown in Figure 8−3*a*.

    b. Beat count 4 because the instrumental parts are playing while the chorus rests. Apply a continuation-attack form (Figure 8−3*b*) for the attack after the downbeat in measure 2.

    c. Treat measure 3 in the same way as the preceding measure.

    d. The continuation attack in Figure 8−6*b* is correct for communicating an off-beat attack after the last beat of a measure.

    e. Substitute a large release loop for beat 4 to obtain a strong phrase release by the chorus.

MUSICAL EXAMPLE 8−3.   **Haydn, The Creation, No. 11, Awake the Harp, beginning measures (Chorus).**

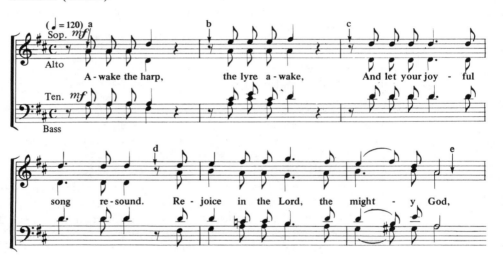

4. Releases, as well as attacks, are important in Musical Example 8−4 for unaccompanied voices. Its style has an element of free delivery (recitative), yet a firm and clear conducting beat is essential. The excerpt is in pentatonic mode (five-note scale: B flat−C−D−F−G) and has a strong phrase structure with accented attacks and sustained endings.

    a. Prepare your initial off-beat attack using the form illustrated in Figure 8−5*a*. Both the ictus point and rebound should be strong to represent an accented *fortissimo* attack.

    b. Keep a *fortissimo* level through the sustained phrase ending and execute a large release loop, filling the entire count's duration, on the downbeat.

Negate beat 2 and give a full preparation for an on-beat attack on count 3 (review Figure 5–8 as an illustration).

c. Activate your left hand in a gesture for more sound (Figure 4–9) during the preceding tied note, then bring both hands into a half preparation for the continuation attack after beat 2 (Figure 8–5b).

d. Use your left hand to assist in communicating the *diminuendo* and bring both hands into a gentle release loop for the final downbeat.

MUSICAL EXAMPLE 8–4. **Randall Thompson, The Peaceable Kingdom, No. VI, Recit. — But These Are They that Forsake the Lord, beginning measures.** Copyright 1936, by E. C. Schirmer Music Co., Boston. Used by permission.

5. Precise and confident attacks are essential in Musical Example 8–5. You can prepare each on-beat attack for the women's voices with your right hand (arrow *a* on beat 3 and arrow *c* on beat 2). Off-beat attacks (after beat 2) in the male voices at arrows *b* and *d* can be prepared and given with both hands together. Attacks on other figures in the male voice parts need no special preparation because rhythmic momentum of words and music will make them happen automatically.

MUSICAL EXAMPLE 8–5. **Handel, The Messiah, No. 44, Hallelujah, measures 51–56 (Chorus).**

Off-Beat Attacks Following a Fermata

You have learned in previous units how to leave fermatas with on-beat attacks. Some fermatas, however, are followed by after-beat attacks. Figure 8–8 illustrates basic techniques for conducting typical musical examples in which a hold occurs on the downbeat of a two-beat pattern (the same techniques can be applied to other beats in other meters). When a complete break is involved, you must give a full release, pause, and go ahead with a half preparation for the next off-beat attack. Other cases, such as those illustrated with form *a*, can be handled ending in a hold position far enough away from the next ictus to enable continuation with a half preparation into that beat. Duration of the fermata ceases at the ictus (no release loops are needed), and the off-beat attack coincides with your rebound. Practice each notated example in Figure 8–8 until you have a feeling for the timing and coordination of all movement. Adjust your hold position, and the form of preparation for the off-beat attack, to fit each musical situation.

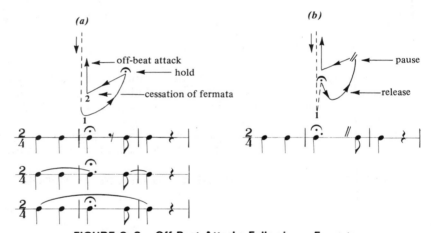

FIGURE 8-8. Off-Beat Attacks Following a Fermata

Musical Example 8–6 contains two examples from Beethoven's Third Symphony that illustrate fermatas left on an off-beat. The first continues without interruption and can be conducted by using form *a* in Figure 8–8, with a modification of the half preparation into a more legato movement as it leaves the hold position. When this same form is applied to the second excerpt, it should have a light staccato stroke and ictus. Release of the fermata by winds will occur at the ictus point, and the off-beat attack in strings at the top of your rebound.

Other After-Beat Attacks

You will recall from Figure 8–1 that after-beat attacks that do not occur exactly as off-beats either precede or follow the midpoint of a beat's duration.

MUSICAL EXAMPLE 8-6. Beethoven, Symphony No. 3 in E Flat Major (Eroica), Movement IV, (*a*) measures 101-107, (*b*) measures 25-35.

Our two kinds of preparatory motion—full and half—serve to communicate these types as well as on- and off-beat attacks. A fundamental rationale can be used to determine which preparation to apply. The response of performers in timing attacks seems to be of such nature as to relate anything starting at, or before, the midpoint to the preceding ictus, and anything after the midpoint is sensed in relation to (in anticipation of) the following ictus. Therefore, use a half preparation to communicate attacks preceding the off-beat and a full preparation to the next beat for attacks following the off-beat. Musical Examples 8-7 and 8-8 illustrate the two situations. Practice each excerpt to test the rationale and apply your technique.

Start Musical Example 8-7 with a small staccato beat directed to the strings, which have very soft, crisp, on-beat attacks. Cue the clarinet and bassoon solo by enlarging your full preparation for the downbeat of measure 3. The correct value of the pick-up eighth note will be felt by you and the players in anticipation of arriving at beat 1, measure 3, in tempo. Maintain a steady two-beat pattern through the rest of the excerpt.

MUSICAL EXAMPLE 8-7. Tchaikovsky, Symphony No. 5 in E Minor, Movement I, measures 40-45.

Musical Example 8-8 uses a half-note beat unit and is conducted two beats per measure. Points labeled *a* and *b* start a pitch-rhythm pattern between the beginning and middle of a beat's duration, leaving a tied note in the first case and following a rest in the second. Your half-preparation stroke into beat 2 must be quick, and the ictus should be pointed. Do you see, and feel, the difference between three straight eighths at arrow *b* and three triplet eighths at arrow *c?* The triplet group falls squarely on an off-beat, and your half preparation at this point probably will feel a little more relaxed compared with that at arrow *b.*

MUSICAL EXAMPLE 8–8. Beethoven, Symphony No. 5 in C Minor, Movement IV, measures 250–254 (Violin 1).

OFF-BEAT ACCENTS AND SYNCOPATIONS

On-beat accents and syncopations were introduced in association with on-beat attacks in Chapter Four. You have had experience in using a full preparation to communicate stresses that occur when sound is attacked with a relatively hard impact at an ictus point. Accents also take place on off-beats. The first rhythmic division of a beat in simple meters is into two equal parts (that is, a quarter-note beat unit first divides into two equal and even parts, represented by eighth notes or rests). This duple division of beats results in three common situations where off-beat accents are found in music. They can occur alone, in succession with an on-beat accent, or as part of a pattern of off-beat rhythmic syncopation.

Conducting patterns can be modified to communicate any of the three kinds of continuation off-beat accents. The basic form and technique includes a straight stroke into the ictus, followed by a straight rebound of sufficient weight to create at its top a feeling of a secondary ictus timed with the off-beat accent. The overall pattern of movement is angular and dynamic. Figure 8–9 shows three conducting patterns in which each stroke, ictus, and rebound is drawn to represent on-beat and off-beat accents. (You should realize that these forms are not the same as divided-beat conducting patterns, to be introduced in the next chapter.)

FIGURE 8–9. Divided-Beat Accents

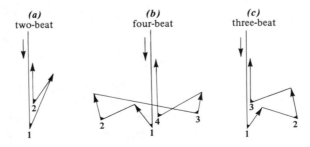

Nonpitch Exercises for Practice

Communicating divided-beat accents within a continuing beat pattern is a matter of substituting, during the accents or syncopation, strokes and rebounds of the kind illustrated in Figure 8–9 and then resuming the ongoing style of beat. The next three nonpitch exercises include drawings of conducting patterns you might use at places involving accents or syncopations. Practice each exercise until you have control of the changing forms in your right-hand beat pattern. You might also want to try activating your left hand for added emphasis at the point of your half preparation entering an off-beat accent or syncopation.

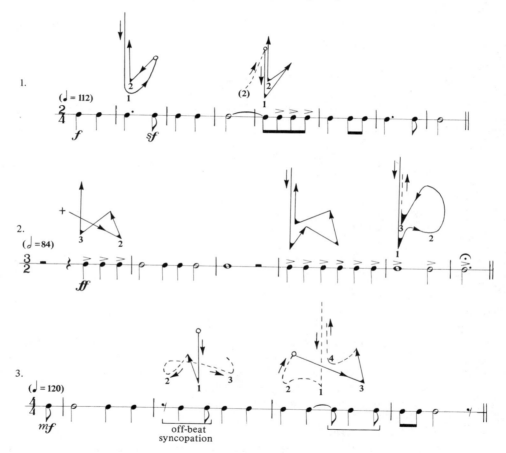

Musical Examples for Study and Practice

Musical Examples 8–9 to 8–14 present an assortment of off-beat accents and syncopations. Study each excerpt in relation to the comments that accompany it, and practice conducting it with the sound of the music in your mind. Your attention to accents and syncopations must be in the total context of all other musical elements for which you are responsible as a conductor.

1. The first measure of Musical Example 8—9 has on-beat accents in the top voice and off-beat accents in those voices written on the middle staff. Conduct the entire measure with a three-beat accented pattern as illustrated in Figure 8—9c. Triplets in measure 2 cannot be treated in the same way. A normal *fortissimo* and marcato three-beat pattern will function better in measure 2 and for the first beat of measure 3. Your beat should smooth out and diminish through the half-note duration.

MUSICAL EXAMPLE 8—9. **Vaclav Nelhybel, Trittico, No. II, measures 77-79 (condensed score).** ©Copyright 1965 by Franco Colombo, Inc. Used by permission.

2. Musical Example 8—10, although only one phrase long, has a variety of marked articulations along with variable tempo and dynamics.

    a. Prepare for a *forte* accented attack on beat 2 and continue for one measure with a marcato-staccato style of beat.

    b. On- and off-beat accents, plus a *ritardando*, can be handled nicely with the divided-beat accent pattern shown in Figure 8—9a.

    c. Resume tempo, and apply a form of beat similar to that illustrated in nonpitch exercise 1, which will represent the off-beat accented eighth note.

    d. Begin a more legato style along with a *diminuendo*.

MUSICAL EXAMPLE 8—10. **Dvořák, edited by Herbert Zipper, English version by Harold Heiberg, Songs of Nature, No. 5, This Day, beginning measures (Soprano).** Copyright, 1952, by Broude Brothers. Used by permission.

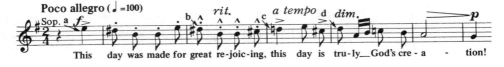

3. Due to its deliberate and martial nature, Musical Example 8–11 contains good opportunities to practice communicating off-beat internal attacks, divided-beat accents, and syncopation.

    a. A half preparation into the ictus of beats marked *a* captures the feeling of firm and precise off-beat attacks on the triplets in measures 1 and 2, and on an eighth-note in measures 3 and 4.

    b. The eighth notes at arrow *b*, although lacking accent marks, are articulated with marcato attacks. The form of beat shown in Figure 8–9*c* works well in the segment starting with beat 2, measure 5, and continuing through measure 6.

    c. Off-beat syncopation over a duration of several beats appears at the end of the theme's repetition. Maintain an angular beat form through this entire segment, for it establishes both a sharp ictus to keep the tempo and an accented rebound to reflect the off-beat rhythmic stress characteristic of syncopation.

MUSICAL EXAMPLE 8–11.   **Tchaikovsky, Symphony No. 4 in F Minor, Movement I, beginning measures.**

4. Musical Example 8–12 begins with a snycopated pattern occupying beats 1 and 2, but the syncopation shifts to beats 3 and 4 in measure 2. You can conduct these patterns in ways very similar to illustrations in nonpitch exercise 3. Start your initial attack with a half preparation into beat 1 (Figure 8–3*a*).

The syncopated patterns in Musical Example 8–12 occur singly (eighth-quarter-eighth) over two beats and are separated by beats which have no syncopation. Those in Musical Example 8–11 are repeated off-beat syncopations (eighth-quarter-

MUSICAL EXAMPLE 8–12.   **Flor Peeters, Jubilate Deo Omnis Terra, SATB.** Copyright ©1954 by McLaughlin & Reilly Company. Used by permission. All rights reserved.

quarter-quarter-quarter-eighth). The two situations should be conducted somewhat differently. In case of a single syncopation, the ictus and rebound following the off-beat accent become normal ones (nonpitch exercise 3). Compare the feeling of this conducting movement with that required for keeping strong ictus points and rebounds through the repeated syncopation in Musical Example 8–11.

5. Conduct the first two measures of Musical Example 8–13 with a marcato-staccato downbeat followed by a tenuto motion—pulling upward—on beat 2 (tenuto style is presented in chapter twelve). Measure 3 is heavy staccato, which is essentially the same as marcato, and measure 4 needs a large phrasing-release loop on beat 2. Sometimes, at faster tempos, repeated syncopation can be handled best by merely keeping a very firm tempo-beat and letting the players or singers set the off-beat stresses against your beat. That situation might be true in this excerpt, starting with measure 5.

MUSICAL EXAMPLE 8–13. **Gustav Holst, Jupiter *from* The Planets, arranged for Military Band, measures 29–35 (condensed score).** ©Copyright 1924 by Boosey & Co.; Renewed 1951. Reprinted by permission of Boosey & Hawkes, Inc.

6. Musical Example 8–14 presents a situation in which a one-measure syncopated pattern (violas, clarinets) in triple meter introduces and accompanies a soft legato melodic line (cellos). Furthermore, the syncopated pattern is *pianissimo* and semistaccato, and it starts with an on-beat attack in the contrabasses. Each of the first two measures can be conducted normally, except you should feel a relatively sharper ictus on beat 1 and a more angular rebound to coincide with the first off-beat attack in the syncopated pattern. Prepare the cello entrance in measure 3 and continue conducting with that melodic line.

MUSICAL EXAMPLE 8–14. **Schubert, Symphony No. 8 in B Minor (Unfinished), measures 42–47.**

NINE

Divided-Beat Patterns and Six-Beat Patterns

In this chapter your experience will be extended in two ways. First, you will find that some music with the same meter signatures you have been conducting in two, three, or four beat patterns will, for very good reasons, require a functional beat unit of less value than those you have been using, and this will result in double or triple the number of beats in each measure. This increase of beats is accomplished in conducting by the technique of dividing each segment of a basic beat pattern into two or three ictus points as appropriate to the meter. Second, you will learn conducting patterns to use in music that moves in six beats per measure, and you will apply forms of six-beat patterns while practicing musical examples.

DIVIDED-BEAT PATTERNS

A divided beat is used when the beat unit in a piece of music has been determined to be a note that represents the first division of the pulse implied by the meter signature. First division in simple meters is a duple division (for example, quarter-note beat units divide into two eighth-note beats), but a triple division occurs in compound meters (for example, a dotted-quarter beat unit divides into three eighth-note beats). Figure 9–1 gives common simple and compound meter signatures with a comparison of their usual and divided applied meanings and their divided-beat conducting patterns.

You must decide during your study and practice of a musical score whether a division of beats is necessary. Tempo is the main determinant. On the basis of correct tempo for the piece, you should select the appropriate beat unit and conducting pattern needed to give the best feeling of control of ensemble precision

Meter	Signature	Usual Applied Meaning	DIVISIONS Applied Meaning	Grouping	Beat Pattern
Simple Duple	**2** 2 or 4	♩ or ♪	♩ or ♪	2+2	divided 2-beat
Simple Triple	**3** 2 or 4	♩ or ♪	♩ or ♪	2+2+2	divided 3-beat
Simple Quadruple	**4** 2 or 4	♩ or ♪	♩ or ♪	2+2+2+2	divided 4-beat
Compound Duple	**6** 4 or 8	(presented separately later in this unit)			
Compound Triple	**9** 8	♩.	♪	3+3+3	divided 3-beat
Compound Quadruple	**12** 8	♩.	♪	3+3+3+3	divided 4-beat

FIGURE 9-1. Divisions of Meters

and flow of the music. Sometimes such a decision is easy. One beat at a rate of 40 per minute may be more difficult to maintain with artistry through an entire piece than two beats at 80, or even three beats at 120 per minute. In other music the correct tempo might seem a little too slow not to divide, but over a long period divided beats could feel uncomfortable. A good maxim is, "Do not use a divided beat if movement in the music can be controlled without division."

Some pieces and movements, or sections thereof, obviously require divided beats throughout because of their very slow tempos—the divided beat unit and conducting pattern are the intended ones. Others can be conducted more effectively with an undivided pattern but may require selective division in places where a *molto ritardando* or after-beat notes of special significance or effect appear. Remember that unnecessary division results in superfluous conducting motion, which conflicts with a normal flow of the music and control of voice lines. When in doubt, practice a passage both with and without division to determine which way works best.

Divided Simple Meters

Division of conducting patterns in simple meters is based on the principle of creating two beats, and ictus points, in each directional segment (down, in, out, and back) of the underlying basic beat pattern. Figure 9-2 illustrates divisions of two-beat, three-beat, and four-beat patterns in simple meter.

Observe, in Figure 9-2, a degree of downward direction into each ictus.

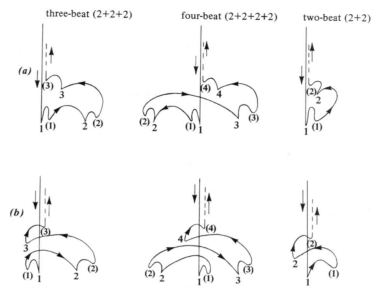

FIGURE 9-2. Divided-Beat Patterns in Simple Meters

Indeed, this is the element of movement that establishes an ictus point and identifies a divided-beat pattern (compare with accented patterns in Figure 8-9). The secondary beat in each direction should be kept near its principal ictus, allowing a longer motion into the next principal ictus and retaining the basic form of the underlying beat pattern. Form *b* for each divided pattern shows certain modifications that can be adapted according to individual preferences. Practice each divided-beat pattern until you can easily maintain its form before continuing with the following musical examples.

Musical examples for study and practice. Conducting music in a divided pattern demands, in addition to an acceptable form, an ability to communicate the same kinds of musical elements you have been attending to while conducting in undivided beats. You must be able to prepare on-beat and off-beat attacks in relation to any principal or secondary ictus, insert release loops, activate the left hand, handle fermatas or rests, and establish a beat representative of the music's style or dynamic level. You also should be able to exercise a degree of flexibility of form within divided-beat patterns in order always to be in a position of movement to make a necessary gesture and then continue the ongoing beat pattern. Musical Examples 9-1 through 9-6 present a variety of situations. Study and practice them until you have sufficient confidence in your technique to control and express the musical qualities of each excerpt.

1. Study the meter signature and metronome marking in Musical Example 9-1. You will conclude that an eighth note functions as the beat unit at a moderate rate of speed, and that a divided two-beat pattern will be required throughout. An Andante tempo in music of eighteenth-century composers, such as Haydn, is very slow and often requires a divided beat. *Andante* in later music usually implies

a moderate tempo. In measure 2 you could give a full release loop, with either hand, on the first eighth note. Continue with minibeats on the rests, and then move into a larger preparation to communicate a *sforzando* attack on the last beat of the measure. Negate the eighth rest in measure 4 and prepare for a phrase attack on the next downbeat. Try to respond in your beat to legato and staccato articulations as they occur.

MUSICAL EXAMPLE 9–1. **Haydn, Symphony No. 104 in D Major, Movement II, beginning measures (Violin 1).**

2. Musical Example 9–2, conducted in a divided two-beat pattern, is a slow introduction to an Allegro movement. The opening fermata should be given a phrasing release ending with a follow-through that will put you in position to stroke downward and inward to the final ictus of the measure where violins start melodic figures. These figures in each successive measure are attacked, following rests, after the principal second beat: after the midpoint in measure 2, at the midpoint (off-beat) in measures 3 and 5, and a little before the midpoint in the triplet pattern in measure 4. Can you make effective preparations for these after-beat attacks (review Chapter Eight as necessary)? The final fermata should be given a final release and pause in observance of the rest and break.

MUSICAL EXAMPLE 9–2. **Beethoven, Symphony No. 1 in C Major, Movement IV, beginning measures.**

3. Musical Example 9–3 presents several challenges; learn the music well before trying to conduct it. Here are the important factors: Start the soft legato melody in first violins, prepare and cue the entrance of lower strings on principal beat 3, release all voices with the downbeat of measure 2, prepare (during the eighth rest) for a *forte* staccato-marcato attack on principal beat 2, employ mini-beats through the end of measure 2, and anticipate repeating the entire process in measures 3 and 4.

MUSICAL EXAMPLE 9–3. **Mozart, Symphony No. 41 in C Major, Movement II, beginning measures.**

4. Musical Example 9–4 contains the broad Adagio ending to a movement that has been moving at a moderate Allegro tempo (see tempo markings in the excerpt). A change from an undivided to a divided beat becomes necessary in cases such as this. A point of tension is reached because of the deceptive cadence on the half-note chord, which can be released with a large loop occupying the full second beat of the chord's duration. Come to a complete pause in observance of the rest marked with a fermata, and then continue with a full preparation for a *forte* attack on principal beat 4 of a divided pattern. Continue your divided beat, plus a left-hand sustaining gesture, through the final measure and substitute a release loop in both hands for the last divided beat of the measure. (This final chord has no fermata marking; therefore, it should not be treated as a hold.)

MUSICAL EXAMPLE 9–4. **Mozart, Requiem, No. 1, Requiem, final measures (Chorus).**

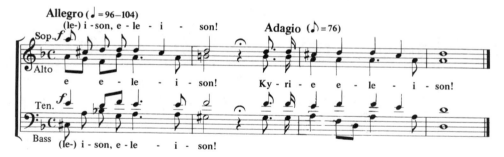

5. Musical Example 9–5 illustrates a tempo in which the conductor might decide to shift between quarter-note beats and divided eighth-note beats according to what is happening in the music. Divided beats function well at the beginning, in response to the marcato style and the predominant rhythmic flow in divisions of the quarter note. Shifting to an undivided beat at the midpoint of measure 3 would be a good way of communicating a more legato flow of sound and a softer dynamic level. Can you prepare attacks following rests in both choral and instrumental parts?

MUSICAL EXAMPLE 9–5. Mozart, Requiem, No. 1, Requiem, measures 15–19.

6. The conclusion of the chorale setting for band in Musical Example 9–6 probably will necessitate going to a division of the two-beat pattern during the *ritardando*, but not until the last half of the next to final measure, where a divided beat will aid in controlling the slowing and accented progression of notes toward the final fermata.

MUSICAL EXAMPLE 9–6. William P. Latham, Three Chorale Preludes for Concert Band, No. III, Now Thank We All Our God, final measures (condensed score). Copyright ©1956 by Summy-Birchard Company. Used by permission. All rights reserved.

Divided Compound Meters

Dotted-note beat units in compound meter divide into three units of equal value (for example, a dotted-quarter equals three eighths; a dotted-half equals three quarters). Consequently, a divided-beat pattern for compound meter must create one principal and two secondary beats, or ictus points, in each directional segment of the underlying conducting pattern. We will reserve special consideration of the six-beat pattern until later and go at this time to nine-beat and twelve-beat patterns, shown in Figure 9–3 as divisions of three- and four-beat patterns, respectively.

Differences of opinion exist as to the best form of nine-beat and twelve-beat patterns. One main issue is whether to move the secondary beats following the primary downbeat in a direction opposite to the next group of three beats (Figure 9–3*a*) and avoid more than three beats in the same direction, or to move the first group of secondary beats slightly toward the next group (Figure 9–3*b*) in order to maintain the clearer underlying pattern created by the three or four principal beats. Either form can work if you keep secondary beats small and close to their principal ictus, and then move with a longer motion in the direction of the next prinicipal ictus. Secondary beats, for that matter, often appear to be at the same point as the principal ictus.

Any principal or secondary beat can be enlarged or moved out of position, if such an action communicates something of musical importance to the ensemble, but a disciplined conductor will return almost immediately to a normal divided-beat form. Although most music based on divided beats in compound meters is in legato style, the change of form to communicate marcato articulations can be done easily whenever such an adjustment becomes necessary. Practice the forms illustrated in Figure 9–3 and experiment with gestures for imaginary attacks, accents, and cues on various beats of each pattern.

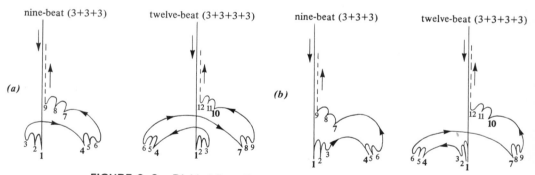

FIGURE 9–3.   Divided-Beat Patterns in Compound Meters

Musical examples for study and practice. Music conducted throughout in a twelve-beat pattern is uncommon, and pieces requiring a continuous nine-beat pattern are rare. Other needs to divide beats in compound meters arise, from time to time: such as a *ritardando* within an ongoing undivided beat; in music with frequent changes from one meter to another (a characteristic of twentieth-century music); and in cases where shifts between divided and undivided beats are feasible.

Because opportunities to conduct music in divided compound meters are infrequent, you may find that your confidence and skill in using them diminishes over time. This can be be overcome by giving additional practice to a score that employs a nine- or twelve-beat pattern. Practice Musical Examples 9–7 through 9–9 to gain initial experiences with music in divided compound meter. You also will find that Musical Example 9–13 contains both a nine-beat and a twelve-beat measure.

1. Musical Example 9–7 moves at a tempo that unquestionably requires a twelve-beat pattern based on an eighth-note beat unit. Attempting to use dotted-quarter beats at a rate of about 34 per minute would prove unmanageable. Try to adjust the form of your beat pattern to the flow of this unison melody, and prepare for precise attacks at the beginning of each phrase and on the first note following notes tied across the bar line between measures 3 and 4. In the latter case, cross the bar line with a small downbeat and rebound into a larger preparatory motion for attack on the next secondary beat.

MUSICAL EXAMPLE 9–7. **Arthur Honegger, King David, No. 19, Psalm of Penitence, measures 2–5 *(Tenori, Bassi)*. Copyright 1925 by Foetisch Freres (S.A.).** Copyright renewed 1952 by Foetisch Freres (S.A.). Used by permission of the E. C. Schirmer Music Co., Boston, sole agents.

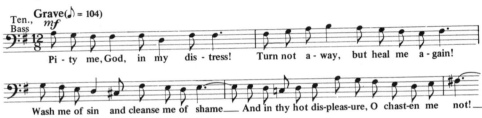

2. The excerpt in Musical Example 9–8 is part of the instrumental introduction to a beautiful alto aria from Bach's St. Matthew Passion. Only the solo violin melody and continuo bass line are quoted, for they provide the essence of what you should respond to as a conductor (a keyboard instrument and other string parts provide the remaining harmony). Continuous eighth-note pulsations in the bass line supply an underpinning for an ornamented melody and establish the same metrical beat as your conducting pattern. Try applying form *a* in Figure 9–3 to this music, and concentrate on communicating the expressive flow of the solo melody within your twelve-beat pattern.

3. Musical Example 9–9 illustrates a situation in which you must make a difficult decision—whether to conduct in four or twelve beats. The instrumental parts provide a persistent rhythmic division of the dotted-quarter beat and for this reason might influence a conclusion that a divided-beat pattern would function best. Chorus parts, on the other hand, can be sustained better with an undivided beat. A rational and artistic choice would be to start the instrumental introduction with a lightly divided beat to establish precision in the eighth-note rhythms, and then to shift to a four-beat pattern as early as the beginning of measure 2, but not later than the entrance of the vocal parts. Of course, options would exist through the entire piece to change back to a divided beat at any time, possibly for only a few beats.

MUSICAL EXAMPLE 9–8. **Bach, St. Matthew Passion, No. 47, Alto Aria with Violin Solo, beginning measures (Violin Solo and Continuo Bass).**

MUSICAL EXAMPLE 9–9. **Mozart, Requiem, No. 7, Lacrymosa, beginning measures.**

SIX-BEAT PATTERNS

Many pieces with meter signatures of six-eight or six-four are conducted with a two-beat pattern because the felt tempo beat is represented by a dotted-quarter or a dotted-half note respectively. You experienced these compound meters in Chapter Seven (Musical Examples 7–4 and 7–6, for example) while developing techniques to apply within the two-beat pattern. The tempo in some music, however, is slow enough to require conducting in a six-beat pattern. An eighth note functions as the beat unit in six-eight, and a quarter note receives one beat in six-four. This follows the same principle as a first division of notes in other compound meters (nine-eight and twelve-eight), but a difference exists in the derivation of the beat patterns used. Whereas nine-beat and twelve-beat patterns are divided three-beat and four-beat forms, the six-beat pattern has its own traditional forms that are independent from a divided two-beat pattern.

Figure 9–4 illustrates several functional conducting patterns that can be applied to music in sextuple meter. Two of these forms show a full six-beat pattern; either one can be employed for conducting pieces that move with a feeling of six beats per measure through their entirety. Other pieces move at a borderline tempo that at times is comfortable in a two-beat pattern, but at other times might call for some kind of divided two-beat form. Figure 9–4 shows a two-beat form and two functional semidivisions of that form. If you add to these one-measure forms combinations of one-half measure of one form with one-half measure of another, you will have the potential to conduct any musical effect encountered in sextuple meter.

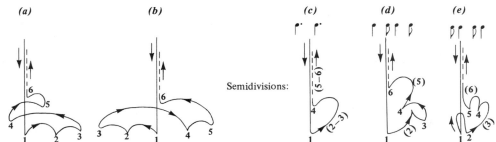

FIGURE 9–4. Conducting Patterns in Sextuple Meter

Similar adaptations of the concept of semidivision can be applied to nine-beat and twelve beat patterns. Practice separately each of the forms in Figure 9–4, and then practice various combinations of halves of forms *c, d,* and *e.*

Musical examples for study and practice. Musical Examples 9–10 through 9–13 provide initial experiences for you to conduct in six-beat patterns and in semi-divisions of a two-beat pattern. In the final excerpt you will have an opportunity to conduct all three divided compound meters in a context of changing meter signatures.

1. Musical Example 9–10 moves at a moderate tempo that can be conducted in a six-beat pattern throughout. Form *b* in Figure 9–4 would function very well because its balance of left and right directions relates directly to division of measures into two three-beat motives. Cue the entrance of each voice line.

2. Try both form *a* and form *b,* Figure 9–4, in conducting Musical Example 9–11. Which form do you prefer for this moderately quick tempo? Which gives you a feeling of better coordination in preparing attacks at entrances of voice lines as well as on the *sforzando* chords?

MUSICAL EXAMPLE 9–10. **Brahms, Symphony No. 4 in E Minor, Movement II, beginning measures.**

MUSICAL EXAMPLE 9–11. **Mozart, Symphony No. 40 in G Minor, Movement II, beginning measures.**

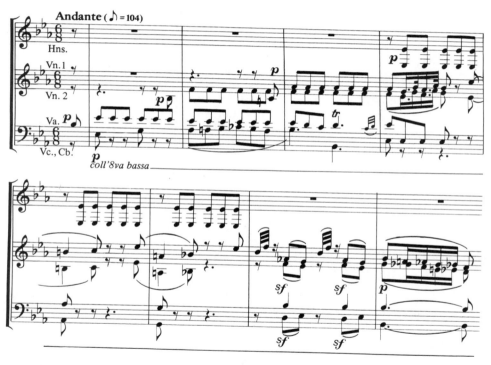

3. Tempo and rhythm patterns in Musical Example 9–12 make it a candidate for a range of fully divided and semidivided beat forms. In this kind of situation form *a* in Figure 9–4 works better for a six-beat pattern because it is allied in its basic directions and form with the two-beat pattern and semidivisions illustrated in forms *c, d,* and *e.* Changes from one to another of these forms are relatively easy. Start the excerpt in a full six-beat pattern and experiment with applying semidivisions in the other measures. Try also to incorporate the variable dynamics into

the shape of your beat pattern. Ultimate decisions on how to conduct each measure must be made by the individual conductor. Generally, semidivision should be kept to a minimum.

MUSICAL EXAMPLE 9–12. **William Walton, arranged by Bram Wiggins, Miniatures for Wind Band, No. 3, beginning measures (Clarinets I and II).** ©Copyright, 1974, by the Oxford University Press, London. Used by permission.

4. Musical Example 9–13 has a different meter signature in each measure, but an eighth note (at the rate of 120 per minute) remains the beat unit throughout. Consequently, measure 1 has six beats, measure 2 has four beats, measure 3 has twelve beats, and measure 4 has nine beats. First, learn the sound of the music in a continuous flow of all parts without concern for changes in meter. Then, conduct with the horizontal flow of music and with correct beat patterns for each measure. You should leave the beginning fermata without an interruption by moving (without a release) from a hold position into a preparatory motion for attack on beat 4 of a six-beat pattern. Finally, conduct the excerpt with a sense of style and dynamics, and give release and attack gestures where you believe they might be needed in each voice line.

MUSICAL EXAMPLE 9–13. **Luigi Zaninelli, Never Seek to Tell Thy Love.** ©Copyright MCMLXIII, Shawnee Press, Inc., Delaware Water Gap, Pa. 18327. Used by permission.

Ten

Irregular Meters and Changing Meters with a Constant Beat Unit

Meters of five and seven beats are fairly common in twentieth-century music but rarely found prior to the late 1900s. They sometimes are called irregular (or asymmetrical) meters because of a combination of duple and triple accent groupings within the same measure. You may also encounter meters of eight, nine, ten, or eleven organized in successions of duple and triple beat groupings per measure in contemporary music. We will examine meters of fives and sevens in some detail, and these will serve to illustrate a fundamental approach to other irregular meters as well.

A basic model for determining conducting patterns in modern fives and sevens includes these steps: (1) Identify the beat unit—kind of note to receive one beat's duration—that will permit control of tempo and precision of ensemble; (2) Determine, for each measure, accent groupings of beats that underline the metrical flow of durations in the voice lines (for example, fives: 2 + 3 or 3 + 2; sevens: 3 + 4, 4 + 3, or 2 + 3 + 2); (3) Use a conducting pattern that will place accent groupings in directional segments so that a longer motion is given to the first beat of each group (see Figures 10–1 and 10–2).

FIVE-BEAT PATTERNS

Figure 10–1 presents the two most frequently encountered accent groupings in five-beat measures, and illustrates the corresponding conducting pattern for each. A longer lateral motion from inside to outside in both patterns divides the groupings of two and three beats. Practice each form of a five-beat pattern before continuing with exercises and examples that follow.

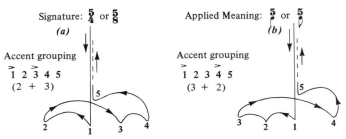

FIGURE 10-1. Five-beat Patterns

Nonpitch Exercises and Musical Examples for Study and Practice

Music that stays in quintuple meter from beginning to end probably will have some measures that fall into a 2 + 3 pattern, some that follow a 3 + 2 grouping, and others that seem to fit either pattern satisfactorily. You must determine which beat pattern to use in each measure rather than depending on only one conducting pattern throughout. Clues to groupings can be found in the relative durations of notes, the way eighth notes are beamed, relative stress on words or word syllables in choral music, and (in some cases) broken bar lines that have been printed between normal bar lines. Continue to conduct the music in one pattern until you see or feel a conflict between sound and movement, in which case a change is probably in order. Mark your score, if necessary, to indicate measures where a change is needed. The nonpitch exercises and musical examples that follow will provide you with experiences in making decisions and conducting in five-beat patterns.

4. A quick overview of Musical Example 10-1 will lead to a judgment that your five-beat pattern should follow a 3 + 2 grouping. An important clue is found in the durational values of dotted-half and half notes in the top voice line.

MUSICAL EXAMPLE 10–1. **Gustav Holst, Mars** *from* **The Planets, arranged for Military Band, beginning measures (condensed score).** ©Copyright 1924 by Boosey & Co.; Renewed 1951. Reprinted by permission of Boosey & Hawkes, Inc.

5. Musical Example 10–2 moves nicely with a five-beat conducting pattern of 2 + 3 (Figure 10–1a). Continue to conduct this excerpt until you can communicate good phrase attacks within your five-beat pattern. The initial attack should receive a full preparation for starting on the last beat of the pattern. Give a full preparatory motion for a downbeat phrase attack in measure 3, and use half preparations to time the off-beat attacks that follow eighth rests.

MUSICAL EXAMPLE 10–2. **Jack Beeson, Homer's Woe, No. 10, beginning measures.** ©Copyright 1967 by Boosey & Hawkes, Inc. Reprinted by permission.

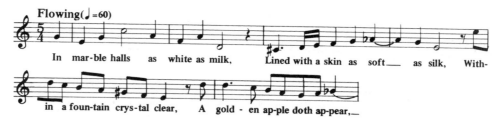

SEVEN-BEAT PATTERNS

Forms

Meter signatures of seven-eight or seven-four require a seven-beat conducting pattern unless the music is at a very fast tempo in which notes of greater value than the eighth or quarter, respectively, function as beat units (fast fives and sevens are presented in the next chapter). Septuple meter in twentieth-century music has the potential for at least four accent groupings and conducting patterns (see Figure 10–2). Seven-beat forms cover all four directions, and beats are distributed within directional segments so that the first beat of a group is entered from a longer motion and change of direction. Study and practice each form illustrated in Figure 10–2.

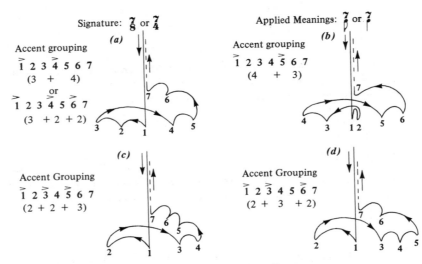

FIGURE 10-2. Seven-Beat Patterns

Nonpitch Exercises for Study and Practice

The next four nonpitch exercises represent various conditions in septuple meter. You should be able to determine accent groupings in each exercise from the notation and rhythm patterns. Select the appropriate seven-beat form in Figure 10–2, and practice conducting each exercise until you can control tempo, dynamics, attacks, accents, rests, and final releases.

CHANGING METERS

Changing meters, symbolized by changes in meter signatures, require corresponding changes in the conductor's beat pattern. Traditional meter changes in music from the Baroque era through nineteenth-century Romanticism occur only between major sections or movements of a composition. This kind of change presents no problem other than the matter of correct tempo relationships.

Choral music of the Renaissance frequently involves meter changes that are the result of the practice of free rhythm found in earlier unbarred plainsong and that was continued in Renaissance part music. Barring in modern editions of this music often requires changes of meter signatures in order to represent the original rhythm as closely as possible (see Musical Example 10–5).

A search for more freedom in rhythm has been part of a greatly expanded exploration of all musical elements by twentieth-century composers; this has brought an extensive use of changing meters into contemporary music. Indeed, meter signatures may change as often as every successive measure through some sections of a piece.

Changing meters are of two types: those that involve a constant beat unit and those that use variable (two) beat units. The first type will be considered here, and the second will be introduced in Chapter Eleven. You should have few problems in conducting music with changing meters in which the same kind of note functions as the beat unit through all meters. The most important factors are to cross the bar line into a new meter with a downbeat and to continue with the appropriate conducting pattern for that measure, and subsequent measures, until another change appears.

Nonpitch Exercises and Musical Examples for Study and Practice

Simple meters, compound meters, divided-beat meters, and irregular meters are all to be found in music characterized by changing meters. You will encounter both traditional and nontraditional ways of writing meter signatures. Modern practices include meter signatures written with only one number to indicate meter (for example, 2, 3, 4), with both numbers directly above a bar line, with a number over a note head, with two signatures at the beginning, or with no signatures. The composer's intentions are easy to interpret in most cases. Study and practice the following nonpitch exercises and musical examples. You already have the necessary knowledge and technique to conduct changing meters with a constant beat unit; all you need is experience.

*A dotted-half note in the new meter has the same duration as a half note in the preceding section: a 50 percent increase in quarter-note beats to 108 per minute.

8. Musical Example 10–3 has changes among simple meters and a metronome marking that identifies a quarter note as the beat unit at a moderate tempo. Play this condensed band score on a piano, then conduct through the changing meters as though the bar lines do not exist. Ignoring bar lines is a good way to sense the music's flow, which changes in meter are supposed to facilitate. Of course, you must establish a downbeat at the beginning of each measure for benefit of the players. Finally, conduct for the shape of the first four-measure phrase, give a timpani entrance cue on the downbeat of measure 4, and execute a phrasing release-attack at the end of measure 4 and beginning of measure 5.

MUSICAL EXAMPLE 10–3. **Donald H. White, Ambrosian Hymn Variants for Band, measures 113–118 (condensed score).** ©Copyright 1968 by Elkan-Vogel Co., Inc. Used by permission.

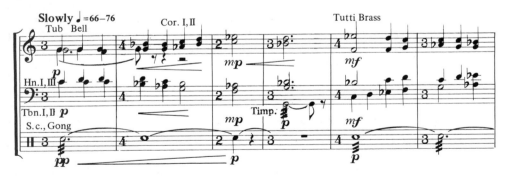

9. Determination of which beat patterns and forms to use in Musical Example 10–4 is easy. Devote your primary attention to conducting the horizontal voice lines. A phrasing release-attack should be given between the two main phrases in the soprano II part. The alto part needs an entrance cue in measure 2 and a phrase

release in measure 4. A second phrase attack in the alto line, and finally an entrance in the soprano I line, should be prepared.

MUSICAL EXAMPLE 10–4. **Jean Berger, Vision of Peace, No. III, beginning measures.** Copyright 1949, Broude Brothers. Used by permission.

10. Musical Example 10–5 is an excellent example of the use of changing meters to capture free-flowing melodic rhythm in a piece of late Renaissance music. This excerpt presents one new situation at the three-eight measures. A note equation above the staff indicates that an eighth note retains the same value as before; hence, you can shift from quarter-note beats at a rate of 54 to eighth-note beats at twice that rate (108). The two measures of triple meter are easy to conduct and control, and they are musically effective. Study each of the three phrases. Can you prepare each phrase attack and communicate expressive phrase shapes?

MUSICAL EXAMPLE 10–5. **Hans Leo Hassler, edited by Herbert Zipper, I Leave Thee Love (Ich Scheid von dir), measures 22–28 (Soprano I).** Copyright 1952, by Broude Brothers. Used by permission.

11. Musical Example 10–6 includes a new irregular meter—eight-eight. Broken bar lines are used to show that the composer intends these measures to be felt in accent groupings of 3 + 3 + 2. You can easily modify form *a* of the seven-beat patterns (Figure 10–2) and make it an eight-beat pattern by adding one secondary beat to the second directional (outside) segment: 3 + 3 + 2 replaces 3 + 2 + 2. Study the last measure of the excerpt, where a conflict of accent groupings (cross

rhythm) exists between the two voice lines. In a case such as this one, keep your basic twelve-beat pattern (a divided four-beat form) and let the viola part play against it while the violins play with it.

MUSICAL EXAMPLE 10–6. **Bela Bartok, Music for Strings, Percussion and Celesta, beginning measures.** ©Copyright 1937 by Universal Edition; renewed 1964. Copyright and renewal assigned to Boosey & Hawkes, Inc. Reprinted by permission.

ELEVEN

Fast Irregular Meters and Changing Meters with Variable Beat Units

Chapter Ten introduced forms of conducting patterns that are used for irregular quintuple and septuple meters whenever the kind of note represented by the meter signature's lower number functions as the beat unit, thus requiring all five or seven beats per measure. In twentieth-century music, however, meters of five and seven often occur at a fast tempo and among changing meter signatures. Conducting fast fives and sevens (as well as other irregular organizations in meters of eight, ten, or eleven) in a context of changing meters is a skill that must be developed in order to handle many works composed since World War II.

FAST IRREGULAR METERS

Forms

Fast irregular meters organize into two or more beat units, each of which represents the total duration of an underlying accent group of two or three divisions of the beat. A plain note (such as a quarter or half note) becomes the beat unit for a duple grouping, and a dotted note (dotted quarter or dotted half) represents a triple grouping. For example, a five-eight measure with an accent grouping of 2 + 3 has a quarter-note beat followed by a dotted-quarter-note beat in the same measure. Each measure of fast fives or sevens has an irregular division that requires a conducting pattern in which one of the beats is longer in duration. Conducting patterns are irregular as a result of creating an ictus only at the beginning of each accent group instead of on each division within the group. Figures 11–1 and 11–2 present essential elements related to conducting patterns for fast fives and sevens, respectively.

147

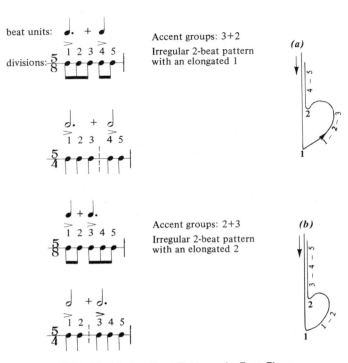

FIGURE 11-1. Beat Patterns in Fast Fives

FIGURE 11-2. Beat Patterns in Fast Sevens

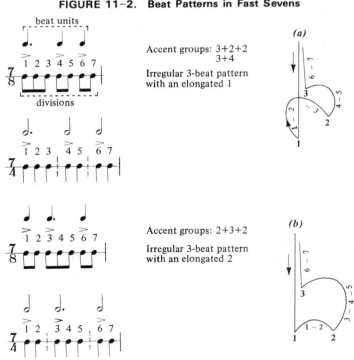

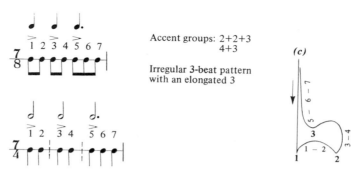

Accent groups: 2+2+3
4+3

Irregular 3-beat pattern
with an elongated 3

(c)

FIGURE 11-2 *cont.*

A few guidelines can serve as a model for practicing your conducting in fast fives and sevens. First, determine from the tempo indications and from the flow of durational patterns whether measures of irregular meter should be conducted in patterns for fast tempos. Second, identify accent groupings and corresponding beat units in each measure; then select the appropriate irregular conducting pattern from those illustrated in Figures 11−1 and 11−2. Third, count out loud, or think, divisions within each accent grouping in order to maintain the relative duration of each beat (keep durations of the divisions equal and even throughout). Finally, practice until the beat patterns are accurate and comfortable.

Nonpitch Exercises for Study and Practice

The next four exercises in fast fives and sevens are written so that you can easily relate metronome markings (shown in representative forms), beat units per measure, divisions of the beats into accent groupings, and rhythm patterns in each measure. Analyze the exercises and select a correct beat pattern, or patterns, for each (Figure 11−1 or 11−2). Next, conduct each exercise while evenly counting the underlying accent groupings. Your elongated beats for dotted-beat units will necessarily involve both longer and slower rebounds to fill the longer durations. Each beat must arrive at its ictus simultaneously with its corresponding accented count. Finally, conduct each exercise while chanting its rhythm with a neutral syllable (*tah* or *lah*).

Changing Meters with Variable Beat Units

Twentieth-century music based on changing meters uses endless mixtures and sequences of fast irregular meters along with simple and compound meters. One of your first jobs in preparing a score is to determine the common unit (note) of division that runs through the entire section or piece. Ordinarily, this common division of the beat will be an eighth note in combinations of simple meters in which four is the lower number— $\frac{2}{4}\frac{3}{4}\frac{4}{4}$ —and fast meters with eight on the bottom— $\frac{2}{8}\frac{3}{8}\frac{4}{8}\frac{5}{8}\frac{6}{8}\frac{7}{8}\frac{8}{8}\frac{9}{8}\frac{12}{8}$. Functional beat units in these cases will vary between a quarter note and a dotted-quarter note. Measures in $\frac{2}{4}\frac{3}{4}\frac{4}{4}\frac{2}{8}$ or $\frac{4}{8}$ contain only quarter-note beats; measures in $\frac{3}{8}\frac{6}{8}\frac{9}{8}$ or $\frac{12}{8}$ have only dotted-quarter (elongated) beats; and measures of irregular meter such as $\frac{5}{8}$ and $\frac{7}{8}$ include both kinds of beat units. The number of conducting beats per measure will range from one to four. Music using combinations of meters such as $\frac{2}{2}\frac{3}{2}\frac{4}{2}\frac{2}{4}\frac{3}{4}\frac{5}{4}\frac{6}{4}\frac{7}{4}$ and $\frac{9}{4}$ share a quarter note as their common divided-beat unit, and the variable beat units become half notes and dotted-half notes. All other factors in conducting these meters are the same as for meters based on variable quarter and dotted-quarter beats.

Occasional exceptions to the preceding assumptions can be found. For instance, three consecutive quarter notes in a measure with a meter signature of six-eight look and sound like a divided accent grouping of 2 + 2 + 2 (not 3 + 3) and should be conducted in three quarter-note beats rather than in two dotted-quarter beats. You must ultimately scrutinize every measure to determine its rhythmic organization and the best way to conduct it. The nonpitch exercises and musical examples that follow will provide some opportunities for you to experience representative situations.

Nonpitch Exercises for Study and Practice

Conducting complex metrical organizations is always a matter of initially intellectualizing the organization and then practicing until the rhythm seems easy, natural, and expressive. Exercises 1 to 6 are in changing meters, and they are written to include all information you need to make correct decisions in regard to tempo, beat units, and conducting patterns. First, practice conducting while counting aloud the underlying accent groupings through all beats and all measures (for example, Exercise 1 begins: 1̄ 2 3̄ 4| 1̄ 2 3̄ 4| 1̄ 2 3 4̄ 5 6| 1̄ 2 3 4̄ 5). Follow this counting procedure by chanting the notated rhythm patterns, and continue practicing until you are in control of and at ease with your conducting.

Musical Examples for Study and Practice

Musical Examples 11–1 through 11–6 include some representative excerpts from band and choral literature composed since 1950. Analyze the metrical organization of each measure in relation to the marked tempo, select appropriate beat patterns for measures of irregular meter from Figures 11–1 or 11–2, and conduct the entire excerpt with accurate rhythm and correct beat patterns. Conduct each excerpt until you can represent all musical factors (tempo, constant and variable dynamics, style, phrase attacks, and releases) within your conducting movements.

1. Musical Example 11–1 is a relatively simple excerpt in a fast five meter that has accent groupings of 2 + 3. The metronome marking for tied eighth notes

is another way of indicating the speed of a quarter note, which represents the first beat's value in each measure. Form *b* in Figure 11–1 will function through all four measures. As soon as you have control of the variable beat pattern, try to shape each two-measure motive according to its dynamic markings, which actually follow the phrase contour.

MUSICAL EXAMPLE 11–1.   **William Walton, arranged by Bram Wiggins, Miniatures for Band, No. 8 (beginning measures).** ©Copyright 1974, by Oxford University Press. Used by permission.

2. Correct accent groupings and corresponding beat patterns are easy to determine for the seven-eight and five-eight measures in Musical Example 11–2. Accent groupings in the six-eight measures are like those found in nonpitch exercise 4, above, and these two measures should be conducted with a pattern of three quarter-note beats (the same as three-four measures). Chanting the words in rhythm is a good way to practice changing meters in vocal music. You should be careful about how to handle the quarter rest in order to guarantee its silence. It can be either negated or given a minibeat and followed with a good preparation for the next attack on beat 2. Decide whether you believe a release gesture is necessary prior to the rest and, if so, how it could be given.

MUSICAL EXAMPLE 11–2.   **Ron Nelson, God Bring Thy Sword *from* What Is Man?, beginning measures (Soprano).** Copyright 1964 by Boosey & Hawkes, Inc. Reprinted by permission.

3. In Musical Example 11–3, two-four measures should be conducted in a pattern of two quarter-note beats, the three-eight measure in one elongated (dotted-quarter) beat, and the five-eight measure with form *a* in Figure 11–1. Practice conducting the two phrases while chanting the words in their correct rhythm and style of articulation, then sing the melody as you conduct it.

MUSICAL EXAMPLE 11–3. **Randall Thompson, Glory to God in the Highest, beginning measures (Soprano).** ©1958, by E. C. Schirmer Music Co., Boston. Used by permission.

4. Musical Example 11–4 has a change in meter for each of its eleven consecutive measures. It is an excellent illustration of the initial need to intellectualize (think through) the metrical organization, then to practice with concentration on underlying accent groupings (counting aloud, if necessary) and, finally, to continue practicing until your conducting movements are governed by thinking and feeling the music and text. Three-four measures contain one dotted-half beat, five-four measures have one half-note and one dotted-half beat, and the four-four measure has two half-note beats.

The initial attack in Musical Example 11–4 is difficult because it is an after-beat attack that occurs before the midpoint of a beat's duration. Your basic technique should be in the form of a half preparation for an attack after the downbeat ictus. A tricky beginning such as this might require giving a one-measure (one dotted-half-note beat in this case) lead into the first measure; it can be executed with a small pulsation, in either hand, given in front of your body and out of view of an audience.

MUSICAL EXAMPLE 11–4. **Jean Berger, It Is Good to Be Merry, beginning measures (Soprano).** ©Copyright MCMLXI by Neil A. Kjos Music Co., Publisher, Park Ridge, Il. Used by permission.

5. An interesting situation arises in the last half of Musical Example 11–5. A three-note pattern of rhythm and articulation starts in a three-eight measure (measure 4) and continues through the next two two-four measures (measures 5 and 6). There are three possible ways to conduct these three measures (4, 5, and 6). You could, of course, do them as barred. Another possibility would be to combine the three measures into one eleven-eight measure conducted in a four-beat pattern comprising three dotted-quarter-note beats and one quarter-note beat (3 + 3 + 3 + 2), which is what the music actually does. A third option would be a one-beat measure

of three-eight followed by combining the two two-four measures into one eight-eight measure of 3 + 3 + 2 conducted in a three-beat pattern. Conductors of twentieth-century music can make such choices so long as they provide an easier coordination of conducting and performance without altering the actual sound of what was written.

MUSICAL EXAMPLE 11-5. **Donald H. White, Patterns for Band, beginning at Letter N.** ©Copyright 1969 by Elkan-Vogel Co., Inc. Used by permission.

6. Study Musical Example 11-6 and make your own decisions about how to conduct it. The excerpt concludes a movement and should have a final release.

MUSICAL EXAMPLE 11-6. **Donald H. White, Miniature Set for Band, No. I, Prelude, final measures (condensed score).** ©Copyright MCMLXIV, Templeton Publishing Co., Inc. Sole selling agent: Shawnee Press, Inc., Delaware Water Gap, Pa. 18327. Used by permission.

Additional Techniques

Chapters One through Eleven have presented foundations of conducting that will enable you to handle almost any musical situation you encounter in music of all styles and periods, with the exception of *avante-garde* compositions. Continued growth in your knowledge and skill will come through increased and deliberate applications of the principles you have learned to a variety of scores over a long period of time. Consideration of a few additional techniques will further improve your ability to communicate musical intent and to control ensemble performance. Remaining skills presented in this chapter include "silent" beats, combined beats, the left-hand gesture for *crescendo e diminuendo*, tenuto articulation, cross rhythm, and hemiola.

SILENT BEATS

The term *passive* is sometimes used to designate conducting motions or gestures that imply only silence and, thereby, nullify any stimulus for an active response by singers or players in an ensemble. Passive gestures include negated beats, minibeats, and "silent" beats. You already have applied techniques for negating beats or for using minibeats to communicate rests with a duration of only one or two counts. Rests of longer duration in all parts (*tutti* rests) can be observed with "silent" beats.

Form

A silent beat pattern shows only direction. It moves in very small straight lines and has no identifiable ictus points. This pattern serves to mark time without asking for any response. Silent beats differ from minibeats to the extent that the latter, although reduced in size, retain the form and expression of a countinuing beat pattern, and they can be used, in certain types of situations, through sustained sound as well as through brief silence.

Skill in applying silent beats involves keeping their small, straight form until the time comes to resume the normal beat pattern with a preparatory motion for an attack of sound following the period of rest. Figure 12-1 illustrates silent forms of three basic beat patterns and preparatory motions for the resumption of active response on beats 3 and 4 of a four-beat pattern. These principles of movement can be transferred to other patterns and other beats.

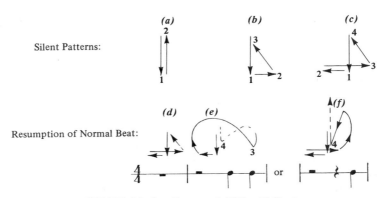

FIGURE 12-1. Forms of "Silent" Beats

Another use for a silent beat arises at measures of *tutti* silence marked with either a fermata sign or the abbreviation **G.P.** (from the German *Grosse Pause,* "long pause"). The duration of these silences is unmetered; therefore, the measure needs only a silent downbeat, rebound, and pause. A preparatory motion for progressing to the next measure should be given after pausing for a duration that gives maximum effect.

Musical Examples for Study and Practice

1. Using a release gesture for the cessation of sound prior to a *tutti* rest of one or more measures is usually a good idea. In Musical Example 12-1, you could execute a left-hand release gesture with the last beat of measure 3. Keep your release motion in the *pianissimo,* legato style of the melody. Continue a right-hand silent beat pattern through beats 1 and 2 of measure 4, then resume active response with a large full preparation for a heavy attack on the downbeat of measure 5. The quarter-note chord in measure 6 can be treated with a right-hand release and followed by regular beats, or minibeats, on the quarter rests. Straight silent beats are less manageable and less appropriate on these two beats of rest because the silence is more active as an integral part of the music's ongoing momentum at this point.

MUSICAL EXAMPLE 12-1. **Schubert, Symphony No. 8 in B Minor (Unfinished), Movement I, measures 59-66 (Strings).**

2. Musical Example 12-2 requires good communication of attacks and releases, as well as correct handling of the measures of silence. Direct your downbeat attack to the instrumental accompaniment, and immediately shift your attention and preparatory beat to the chorus for its entrance on beat 2. The second beat of measure 2 should be a release gesture (in either hand or in both hands) to the chorus. Continue two measures of silent right-hand beats, using the last one to extend into a full preparation for a downbeat attack in the accompaniment. This excerpt comprises the ending of a movement that has two final measures of silence. You should keep a silent beat through the entire duration, for the silence was conceived as part of the music's conclusion, not as a postending.

MUSICAL EXAMPLE 12-2. **Mendelssohn, Elijah, No. 13, Call Him Louder, final measures.**

COMBINED-BEAT GESTURES

Form

A combined-beat gesture is one that blends or melds two or more beats into one longer motion that occupies the same duration individual beats would take. The gesture creates an ictus for the first of the combined beats, continues unbroken in a general direction for the melded beat or beats without forming an ictus for them, and strokes clearly into an ictus for the beat following the merged counts. Your movement through melded beats must be slower to fill their combined duration, and you must maintain accurate duration to prepare for the next ictus at its exact point in time. Figure 12–2 shows some possibilities for combining beats in a four-beat pattern and a gesture for melding a complete measure in any meter. These principles can be applied within all beat patterns.

Combined-beat gestures are particularly effective and expressive in sustaining the intensity of tones of longer duration through short *crescendos,* at midpoints of phrases, or at ends of phrases where they terminate in a release loop. They also coordinate well, under certain conditions, with the flow of sound through a durational pattern that would be disturbed by showing all ictus points (see cross rhythms, Figure 12–4). You should fully realize that a combined-beat gesture is unlike a fermata because its duration is exactly as notated, and movement continues without stopping in a hold position.

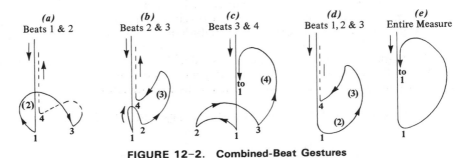

FIGURE 12–2. Combined-Beat Gestures

Musical Examples for Study and Practice

Musical Examples 12–3 and 12–4 illustrate places in a melodic line where a conductor might opt in favor of combining beats. Musical Examples 12–7 and 12–14, cited later in this chapter, also contain potentials for melded-beat gestures.

1. Musical Example 12–3 constitutes an opening four-measure melodic phrase that should be sung with an unbroken arch contour. Application of a combined-beat gesture through beats 3 and 4 (Figure 12–2) in measure 2 will supply a physical and psychological stimulus for stretching the half note and thus help avoid a tendency of most singers to fade or break at the phrase's midpoint.

MUSICAL EXAMPLE 12–3. **Mendelssohn, Elijah, No. 29, He Watching Over Israel, beginning soprano part.**

2. Melding beats 1 and 2 during the half note in measure 4 of Musical Example 12–4 can be an effective way of communicating the *crescendo* from *piano* to *forte*. To do this, you must increase the size and weight of your movement through the combined-beat gesture and through the stroke into an attack ictus on beat 3. Addition of your left hand through this entire gesture is a workable option.

MUSICAL EXAMPLE 12–4. **Tchaikovsky, Symphony No. VI in B Minor (Pathetique) Movement I, measures 89–95 (Violin 1).**

CRESCENDO-DIMINUENDO GESTURE

One of the most important functions of the left hand is to assist in communicating variable dynamics. You have had a number of opportunities thus far to activate your left hand in gestures for more sound, less sound (*subito piano*), *crescendo*, and *diminuendo*. Control of movement through a gradual increase in loudness followed immediately by a gradual decrease (*crescendo e diminuendo*) is one of the more difficult independent gestures for the left hand, and one that usually requires a great deal of practice.

Form

Performance of a *crescendo e diminuendo* gesture can be accomplished by following this sequence of actions: Activate the left hand at approximately waist level (palm facing upward and inclined slightly inward); gradually raise the hand during the *crescendo*, until it reaches its highest level at the peak of loudness; turn the hand over slowly, with palm facing the ensemble, and gradually lower it during the *diminuendo*. A well-executed gesture requires smooth, continuous, and unpulsed movement. Your right-hand beat pattern must continue, although its size and weight will vary with the dynamic changes.

A good way to practice an independent left-hand gesture for *crescendo e diminuendo* is to begin by using the left hand alone over a two-measure span of time in triple or quadruple meter. Count the beats at a moderate tempo while you raise your hand gradually to the point of count 1 in the second measure, smoothly turn the hand over, and let it descend through counts 2 and 3. After this independent movement is well coordinated, add a right-hand beat pattern and continue to practice until both hands function together easily. Finally, apply your skill in musical situations, such as the one in Musical Example 12–5.

Musical Examples for Study and Practice

1. There is no one correct way of conducting Musical Example 12–5 (nor many other examples). Nevertheless, each of the two phrases is shaped by a *cres-*

cendo and *diminuendo*, thereby providing an excellent context for application of a left-hand gesture to communicate that contour. You can experiment with variations in your exact implementation of the gesture. At what points will you activate and deactivate your left hand? How can your right hand function most effectively? What combination of movements in the two hands coordinates most artistically?

MUSICAL EXAMPLE 12-5. **Mendelssohn, Symphony No. 3 in A Minor (Scotch), beginning measures (Oboe 1).**

2. Musical Example 12-6 contains an interesting dynamic effect. The music builds through a series of one-measure *crescendos* from a beginning at triple *piano* to a *forte* level prior to a fermata pause. Although no *crescendo e diminuendo* is involved, a situation where one *crescendo* follows another gives you an opportunity to practice using your left hand to help communicate variable dynamics. You might think of the *crescendos* as having a telescoped effect: Expand one, fall back slightly to start the next, and build it beyond the previous peak. A telescoped treatment sometimes offers a better chance for achieving a gradual increase, rather than a too abrupt one, over a relatively prolonged *crescendo*.

Different conductors might communicate the *crescendos* in Example 12-6 in various ways. Here is one way for you to practice them: Activate your left hand at the beginning of measure 4 on the first *joy*; raise the hand a few inches to cor-

MUSICAL EXAMPLE 12-6. **Randall Thompson, The Peaceable Kingdom, No. VI, For Ye Shall Go Out with Joy, beginning measures (Chorus I).** Copyright 1936, by E. C. Schirmer Music Co., Boston. Used by permission.

respond to the first two-beat *crescendo*; let the hand fall back slightly to start an attack at measure 5, and move it higher through that *crescendo*; do the same to start the final tone, and keep your left hand moving higher and to the outside toward a full extension, which can be terminated with a release loop in conjunction with the right hand. Your right-hand beat should increase in size during the *crescendos*, particularly the last one. You may also try other ways to conduct this excerpt. How could you signal releases prior to the rests?

TENUTO BEATS

Style and Form

Tenuto (held, or sustained, for full value) is actually another style of articulation, affecting one note or a few notes in which sounds connect in a very cohesive manner sometimes explained as *heavy legato*. Tenuto notes are written with the abbreviation *ten.* over them, or with a sign in the form of a straight line over or under the note heads. The abbreviation is usually reserved for use when a single note is involved, but line markings are found with either single notes or a succession of notes.

Tenuto conducting beats should be employed when one or more tenuto articulations are to be performed. This form of movement is variously described as a heavy "paintbrush" stroke, stretching strong rubber, or pulling the hand through water. Three elements characterize a tenuto beat: Each stroke pulls in essentially a straight line; a slight arrest replaces the rebound at each ictus; and the wrist leads the tip of the baton (or tips of fingers) at each change of direction and through each stroke. Figure 12-3 illustrates a four-beat pattern in tenuto style; other beat patterns would adopt a similar form.

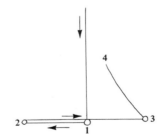

FIGURE 12-3. Tenuto Beats

Musical Examples for Study and Practice

Legato, marcato, or staccato articulations can encompass any duration from one or two notes to an entire piece, with the result that a conductor may stay in one of the basic styles of beat for long periods in some pieces and for only a few beats at a time in others. Tenuto articulation rarely exceeds two measures in any instance, and the conductor encounters quick interchanges between tenuto and other beat styles. Musical Examples 12–7 and 12–8 are somewhat typical.

1. In Musical Example 12–7, tenuto beats follow legato beats. They also start at a louder (*mezzo forte*) level and diminish through the five-beat duration. Conduct this excerpt with attention to beat style, dynamics, and preparations for phrase attacks.

MUSICAL EXAMPLE 12–7. **Tchaikovsky, Symphony No. 5 in E Minor, Movement I, beginning measures (Clarinets).**

2. Tenuto beats at the beginning of Musical Example 12–8 give way to legato beats at count 4 of measure 2. This change is executed by rebounding from ictus points and applying curved shapes to the strokes. Try to conduct the excerpt with attention to all of its elements. Direct the opening attack to the first-horn solo; cue the third-horn solo on beat 1 of measure 2, and the baritone solo on beat 2 in measure 3; change to a legato beat in measure 3; start a *diminuendo* in measure 4; cue the entrances of low woodwinds on beat 1 in measure 4, timpani on beat 2, and high woodwinds on beat 4.

MUSICAL EXAMPLE 12–8. **Donald H. White, Miniature Set for Band, No. II, beginning measures (condensed score).** ©Copyright MCMLXIV, Templeton Publishing Co., Inc. Sole Selling Agent: Shawnee Press, Inc., Delaware Water Gap, Pa. 18327. Used by permission.

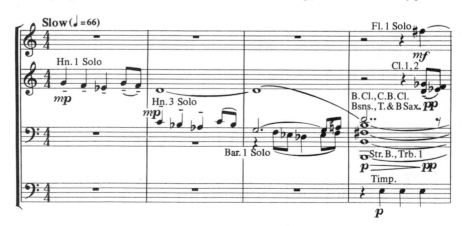

CROSS RHYTHM

Cross rhythm is the simultaneous use of contrasting rhythms in different voice parts. In its broadest meaning, the term is more or less synonomous with *polyrhythm*, which can be interpreted to mean rhythmic independence of individual parts in contrapuntal textures. We will consider more limited and specific illustrations of cross rhythm of two types that exist primarily for their own effects: conflicting (contrasting) patterns within the same meter or accent grouping, and conflicting rhythms resulting from simultaneous meters (called polymetric).

Form

The most common patterns of contrasting rhythms within the same meter are those created when three notes sound against two of the same kind (a 3:2 relation). A 3:2 cross rhythm causes no problem for the conductor when the duration is one beat, for all that is needed is to keep an ongoing beat pattern and let players or singers perform their individual patterns with the beat. When a triplet rhythm occurs over a two-beat duration, a closer analysis is required to make wise decisions about conducting those beats.

Figure 12–4 illustrates three musical contexts in which a two-beat triplet might be found and shows three options for conducting patterns. Figure 12–4*a* has the triplet, in all voice parts, sounding against two beats within the same meter. In such cases, especially at slower tempos, you can continue the regular beat pattern, or you can divide the two metrical beats into three conducting beats that correspond to the triplet rhythm. Ensemble precision, as well as rhythmic expressiveness, can sometimes be handled better with a triplet division of two beats (Musical Example 12–9). If the triplet occurs in a different part of the measure, merely transfer the triplet division to the corresponding part of your conducting pattern.

FIGURE 12–4. Options for Conducting 3:2 Cross Rhythms

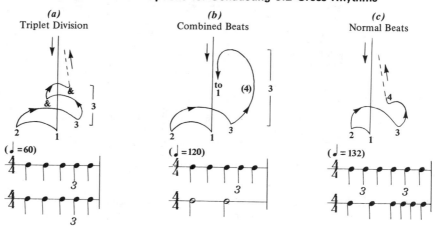

163

Figure 12–4*b* presents a two-beat triplet in one voice against sustained sound in another. Although this rhythm could be conducted in any of the three ways shown, combining two beats into one melded gesture permits the triplets to be performed over the duration of one motion, which causes less conflict than performing them against two beat motions. Option *b* is sometimes a good choice, especially at faster tempos (Musical Example 12–10*a*).

When two-beat triple and duple divisions exist simultaneously, as in Figure 12–4*c*, you must sustain a regular beat pattern. Emphasizing beats where the parts are together (beats 1 and 3) and minimizing motion on the other beats (2 and 4) will make coordination somewhat easier for the conductor and performers alike (see Musical Example 12–10*b*).

The second type of cross rhythm, where conflicting patterns exist because of different simultaneous meters, can be created by using different meters and meter signatures, or by writing different accent groupings in the same meter. Two rather easily handled excerpts of these kinds are quoted in Musical Examples 12–11 and 12–12. More complex cases of polymeter can be postponed until you are ready for more advanced study in conducting.

Musical Examples for Study and Practice

1. Musical Example 12–9 is for unaccompanied chorus. The two-beat triplet rhythm, at a slow tempo and in a deliberate style, adapts very well to a triplet division of the last half of your four-beat pattern, as illustrated in Figure 12–4*a*.

MUSICAL EXAMPLE 12–9. **Randall Thompson, The Peaceable Kingdom, No. VII, Have Ye Not Known, measures 7–9.** Copyright 1936, by E. C. Schirmer Music Co., Boston. Used by permission.

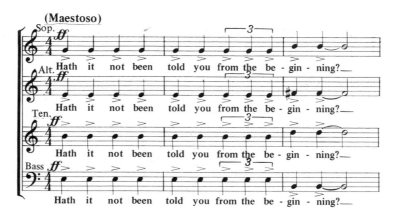

2. Musical Example 12–10 quotes two excerpts (*a* and *b*) from the same work. Relate your conducting of the triplet rhythm, in its context in each excerpt, to forms illustrated in Figure 12–4*b* and *c*.

MUSICAL EXAMPLE 12-10. Fritz Velke, Concertino for Band, No. I, (a) beginning measures, (b) measures 13-14 (condensed score). ©MCMLXII, Templeton Publishing Co., Inc. Sole Selling Agent: Shawnee Press, Inc., Delaware Water Gap, Pa. 18327. Used by permission.

3. You will encounter polymeter in Musical Example 12-11. The same meter signature (twelve-eight) appears in all parts, but the instrumental part moves in a duple accent grouping while the vocal part flows along in triple accent groupings. An eighth note functions as the beat unit for all parts. The instrumental part looks like six-four meter, which could be conducted alone in a divided (duple) six-beat pattern, whereas the vocal part could be conducted alone with a divided (triple) four-beat pattern. How should it be conducted when the parts are performed together? Here is an answer that will work quite well: Begin the one-measure instrumental introduction with twelve beats in the form of a divided six-beat pattern, and shift to a standard twelve-beats per measure, in the form of a divided four-beat pattern, with the entrance of male voices. Rhythmic inertia in the instrumental part, established firmly in the first measure, will enable the player, or players, to continue undisturbed when you shift your main attention to conducting the vocal melodic line. All parts come together rhythmically at the beginning and midpoint of each measure; therefore, it is a good idea to stress the primary beats on 1 and 3 and to minimize all other beats.

4. Musical Example 12-12 is polymetric. Some parts are written in compound duple meter (six-eight) and others in simple triple meter (three-four). Yet, the conductor's job is relatively easy because the music can be conducted one beat per measure in one-beat patterns.

MUSICAL EXAMPLE 12–11. **Arthur Honegger, King David, No. 19, Psalm of Penitence, beginning measures.** ©Copyright 1925 by Foetisch Freres (S.A.). Copyright renewed 1952, by Foetisch Freres (S.A.). Used by permission of the E. C. Schirmer Music Co., Boston, their sole agents.

MUSICAL EXAMPLE 12–12. **Gustav Holst, Second Suite in F, No. IV (condensed score).** ©Copyright 1922 by Boosey & Co., Ltd. Renewed 1949. Copyright and renewal assigned to Boosey & Hawkes, Inc. Reprinted by permission.

HEMIOLA

Hemiola is a term applied to time values in the relationship of 3:2. Use of the term grew out of treatises on music notation in the fifteenth and sixteenth centuries. Hemiola patterns of rhythm became common practice in Baroque vocal music, were a device frequently employed by Brahms, and are still used in twentieth-century music.

Patterns

Typical hemiola patterns are shown in Figure 12–5. The basic principle of hemiola in modern notation is a metrical shift from six-four to three-two, or from

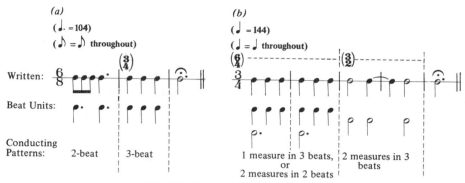

FIGURE 12-5. Hemiola Patterns

six-eight to three-four. Reversal of the metrical shift (such as three-four to six-eight) is also possible. The resulting rhythmic effect is one of change from triple to duple accent groupings, or vice versa, and this change is accomplished by writing appropriate note values in the same meter rather than changing meter signatures (see Figure 12-5). In most cases, a conductor should change his beat pattern with the change of meter produced by hemiola rhythm and should inform the ensemble how that measure, or measures, will be conducted. Study and practice the changes illustrated in Figure 12-5. Musical Examples 12-13 and 12-14 provide further experiences in recognizing hemiola at sight in music scores and offer opportunities to practice conducting representative patterns excerpted from pieces of music.

Musical Examples for Study and Practice

1. Hemiola is an effective compositional device for approaching an important cadence, such as the concluding cadence in Musical Example 12-13. In the next to final measure, change from a two-beat pattern with a dotted-quarter-note beat unit to a three-beat pattern with a quarter-note beat unit (see Figure 12-5a). Keep eighth-note values the same, but execute a *ritardando* within the hemiola measure.

MUSICAL EXAMPLE 12-13. **Knut Nystedt, Cry Out and Shout, final measures.** Copyright ©1956 by Summy-Birchard Company. Used by permission. All rights reserved.

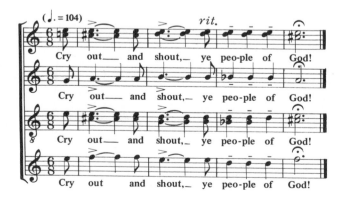

2. Can you locate at sight the hemiola in Musical Example 12–14? Change from a quick three-four beat pattern to a three-two pattern (Figure 12–5*b*) for measures 5 and 6. You also must communicate tenuto style along with a slight *ritardando* and *crescendo* through these measures. The dotted-half note that ends the phrase is an excellent place to apply a combined-beat gesture for the entire measure and terminate it with a phrase-release loop on count 3. Try conducting this entire excerpt.

MUSICAL EXAMPLE 12–14.   **Jean Berger, Vision of Peace, No. II, measures 139–146.** Copyright 1949, by Broude Brothers. Used by permission.

Clefs

Instrumental and vocal parts in conductor's scores are written in the various clefs, which include treble (G) clef, bass (F) clef, and C clefs. Understanding the clefs and their interrelatedness is a prerequisite to studying and reading the score.

The treble-clef sign locates the pitch of G above middle C on the second staff line, and the bass-clef sign identifies the fourth staff line as F below middle C. A C-clef sign "points" to a line or space that is to be named middle C. Theoretically, any staff line or space could be used as middle C, but the fourth-line *tenor clef,* third-line *alto clef,* and first-line *soprano clef* shown below are the most traditional of the C clefs.

1. Comparative clefs and staff locations of Middle C:

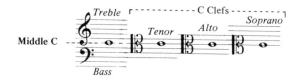

2. C-clef uses and pitch identifications:

a. The tenor clef is sometimes used to write the higher notes found in cello, trombone, and bassoon parts; it is also employed for the tenor voice part in (a very few) choral scores that use the C clefs for soprano, alto, and tenor parts. Positive pitch and octave identifications are shown in staff notation. (Lower case letters represent pitches in the octave below middle C, an offset number 1 indicates pitches in the octave extending upward from middle C, and an offset 2 identifies pitches in the second octave above middle C.)

b. Viola parts, and the first trombone part in some European editions of orchestral scores, are written in the alto clef. Choral scores that use the C clefs probably will have the alto voice part written in the alto clef.

c. Soprano voice parts in choral scores with C clefs are the only cases in which a conductor might encounter the soprano clef.

3. The vocal tenor clef:

The tenor voice part in choral scores using treble clef for soprano and alto parts will be written in a clef with one of three forms of the treble-clef sign: a traditional treble-clef sign, a treble-clef sign with an 8 (8va) attached below, or a double treble-clef sign. In all three cases, middle C is located on the third space, and pitches sound an octave lower in comparison with other parts written in the treble clef.

TRANSPOSITIONS

Transposing instruments are those which sound pitches that are different from the pitches notated in the score; nontransposing instruments are those which sound the pitches that are written. Transposing instruments can be categorized as those that sound at the interval of an octave from the written pitches and those for which the interval of transposition is one other than the octave.

Studying a conductor's score requires the ability to read, think, and sometimes produce the sound represented by each note in the score. This acutal pitch is called *concert pitch*, and it is the same pitch that would be played on a piano. The following lists include both nontransposing and transposing instruments and voices along with the intervals of transposition.

Nontransposing Instruments

1. Those that sound as written in the treble clef:

   Flute
   Oboe

   Violin
   Soprano and Alto voices

2. Those that sound as written in the bass clef:

   Bassoon
   Tenor trombone
   Bass trombone
   Cello

   Euphonium (Baritone)
   Tubas in E♭ and BB♭
   Bass voice

3. Those that sound as written in a C clef:

Viola
Cello, bassoon, trombone, and
vocal parts, which sometimes
might be written in a C clef

Octave Transpositions

1. Those which sound one octave higher than written:

Piccolo in C	Xylophone
Chimes	Celesta

2. Those which sound two octaves higher than written:

Glockenspiel

3. Those which sound one octave lower than written:

Contrabassoon
String Bass (Contrabass)
Male Voice (when written in the treble clef)

Transpositions at Other Intervals

Instrument	Interval of Transposition	Written Note	Actual Sound
Piccolo in D♭	up a minor ninth		
English Horn in F	down a perfect fifth		
Soprano Clarinet in E♭	up a minor third		
Clarinet in B♭	down a major second		
Clarinet in A	down a minor third		
Alto Clarinet in E♭	down a major sixth		
Bass Clarinet in B♭	down a major ninth		
Bass Clarinet in A	down a minor tenth		
Bass Clarinet in E♭	down one octave plus a major sixth		

Instrument	Interval of Transposition	Written Note	Actual Sound

Contrabass Clarinet in B♭ — down two octaves plus a major second

French Horn — (see notated intervals)

The numerous horn transpositions encountered in orchestral scores result from parts written prior to the invention of valve mechanisms for horns and trumpets. In the eighteenth and early nineteenth centuries, removable "crooks" of various lengths of tubing were used to change the horn's construction to one of the fundamental keys in which pitches following the natural overtone series could be played (octave, fifth, second octave, third, fifth, seventh, and continuing upward scalewise).

Trumpet or Cornet in B♭ — down a major second

Trumpet or Cornet in A — down a minor third

Trumpet in D — up a major second

Soprano Saxophone in B♭ — down a major second

Alto Saxophone in E♭ — down a major sixth

Tenor Saxophone in B♭ — down a major ninth

Baritone Saxophone in E♭ — down one octave plus a major sixth

Bass Saxophone in B♭ — down two octaves plus a major second

INSTRUMENTATION

Reading conductors' scores for orchestral and band works requires three areas of knowledge regarding identification of the specific instruments used in the composition and the location of their parts in the score: 1) vertical order of instrumental parts from top to bottom in the printed score, 2) instrument names and abbreviations in the four languages most likely to be used (English, German, French, Italian), and 3) names of modes and scale degrees (pitches) in the same four languages.

The full name and key of construction (e.g., Clarinets in A, or Clarinetti in la) are printed to the left of each instrument's staff at the beginning of each piece and movement. Labeling at other places in the score is usually done with corresponding abbreviations.

Traditional Order of Instruments in the Score

Orchestra	Band
Piccolo	Piccolo
Flutes 1, 2	Flutes 1, 2
Flute 3	Oboes 1, 2
Oboes 1, 2	Soprano Clarinet
English Horn	Clarinets 1
Clarinets 1, 2	Clarinets 2
Alto Clarinet	Clarinets 3

Orchestra

Bass Clarinet
Bassoons 1, 2
Contrabassoon
French Horns 1, 2
French Horns 3, 4
Trumpets 1, 2, 3
Cornets
Trombones 1, 2
Trombone 3
Tuba
Timpani
Percussion
Harp
Violins 1
Violins 2
Violas
Cellos
Double Basses

Band

Alto Clarinet
Bass Clarinet
Alto Saxophones 1, 2
Tenor Saxophone
Baritone Saxophone
Bassoons 1, 2
Cornets 1
Cornets 2, 3
Trumpets 1, (2)
Trumpets 2, (3)
Trumpets 3, (2)
French Horns 1, 2
French Horns 3, 4
Trombones 1, 2
Trombones 3
Baritones Horns
Basses
Timpani
Percussion

Instrument Names and Abbreviations

Abbreviations	English	German	French	Italian
Picc., Fl. Picc., Kl. Fl.	Piccolo	Klein Flöte	Petite Flûte	Flauto Piccolo
Fl., Fl. gr.	Flute	Grosse Flöte	Flûte	Flauto
Ob., Hb.	Oboe	Hoboe, Oboe	Hautbois	Oboe
E. H., C. A., Cor. ingl.	English horn	Englisches Horn	Cor anglais	Corno inglese
Cl., Kl.	Clarinet	Klarinette	Clarinette	Clarinett
B. Cl., Bkl., Cl. B.	Bass clarinet	Bass Klarinette	Clarinette basse	Clarinetto basso
Bn., Bsn., Fg.	Bassoon	Fagott	Basson	Fagatto
C. Bsn. Cfg., C. Fag.	Contrabassoon	Kontrafagott	Contrebasson	Contrafagotto
Hn., Hr., Cor.	French horn	Horn, Hörner	Cor, Cor-à-pistons	Corno
Tpt., Tr.	Trumpet	Trompete	Trompette	Tromba
Crnt., Kor.	Cornet	Kornett	Cornet	Cornetto
Trb., Tbn., Pos.	Trombone	Posaune	Trombone	Trombone
Tb., Btb.	Tuba (Bass Tuba)	Tuba (Basstuba)	Tuba (Tuba basse)	Tuba (Tuba di basso)
Timp., Pk.	Timpani (pl.)	Pauken (pl.)	Timbales (pl.)	Timpani (pl.)
Sn. Dr., S.D., C.C.	Snare Drum	Trommel	Caissa claire,	Piccolo cassa
Tamb. milit.			Tambour militaire	Tambouro militare

Abbreviations	English	German	French	Italian
B. Dr., Gr. Tr., Gr. Cassa	Bass Drum	Grosse Trommel	Grosse caisse	Gran cassa
Cymb., Bck., Ptti.	Cymbals (pl.)	Becken (pl.)	Cymbales (pl.)	Piatti (pl.)
Trgl.	Triangle	Triangel	Triangle	Triangolo
Tmbn., Tamb.	Tambourine	Tamburin, Schellentrommel	Tambour de Basque	Tamburino
Hpe., Arp.	Harp	Harfe	Harpe	Arpa
Piano, P.-f.	Piano	Klavier	Piano	Pianoforte
Vl., Vn., Vln.	Violin	Violine	Violon	Violino
Va., Vla., Br.	Viola	Bratsche	Alto	Viola
Vc., Vlc.	Cello	Violoncello	Violoncelle	Violoncello
Cb., C.B., Kb.	Double bass	Kontrabass	Contrebasse	Contrabasso
Sax.	Saxophone	Saxophon	Saxophone	Sassofone
Bar., Eph.	Baritone	Baryton	Baryton	Flicorno tenore
	Euphonium	Euphonion	Basse à pistons	Eufonio

Names of Modes and Pitches

English	German	French	Italian
major	dur	majeur	maggiore
minor	moll	mineur	minore
C	C	ut	do
C-sharp	Cis	ut dièse	do diesis
D-flat	Des	re bémol	re bemolle
D	D	re	re
D-sharp	Dis	re dièse	re diesis
E-flat	Es	mi bémol	mi bemolle
E	E	mi	mi
E-sharp	Eis	mi dièse	mi diesis
F-flat	Fes	fa bémol	fa bemolle
F	F	fa	fa
F-sharp	Fis	fa dièse	fa diesis
G-flat	Ges	sol bémol	sol bemolle
G	G	sol	sol
G-sharp	Gis	sol dièse	sol diesis
A-flat	As	la bémol	la bemolle
A	A	la	la
A-sharp	Ais	la dièse	la diesis
B-flat	B	si bémol	si bemolle
B	H	si	si
B-sharp	His	si dièse	si diesis
C-flat	Ces	ut bémol	do bemolle

Topical Index

Index to Figures and Practice Exercises

(Each figure is listed with its compound number and page. Italicized compound numbers indicate figures which include line drawings of conducting movements along with notated nonpitch patterns for application and practice. Other nonpitch exercises are listed with page references under *Practice*.)

Index to Musical Examples

(Each example is identified with its compound number and page; all are musical illustrations for the application and practice of specific conducting techniques.)